ENGLISH
KnowHow
Student Book 3

Angela Blackwell · Therese Naber

with Gregory J. Manin

OXFORD
UNIVERSITY PRESS

Contents

Contents

Listening / Speaking	Reading / Writing	*KnowHow*
➤ **Listening:** • The Brooklyn Bridge • Features of cars • Song – "Fun, Fun, Fun" ➤ **Speaking:** • Planning a public park • Role-play – Buying / selling a car	➤ **Reading:** *Engineering Challenges* ➤ **Writing:** Describing a public place	➤ Silent consonants
➤ **Listening:** • An errand-running service • Radio commercials ➤ **Speaking:** • Creating a service • Planning a radio commercial	➤ **Reading:** • *Motion Ads May Make Commute Seem Faster* • *Sandwich Boards in Danger* ➤ **Writing:** • A formal letter • A radio commercial	➤ Vocabulary learning
➤ **Listening:** • A surprising story • A radio program about science ➤ **Speaking:** • Describing a frightening or surprising experience • A science quiz	➤ **Reading:** • *Mysteries of the Southwest* • *Unraveling the Mysteries of Fossils* ➤ **Writing:** A frightening or surprising experience	➤ Vowel sounds and spelling
➤ **Listening:** • A soap opera • Are manners going out of style? ➤ **Speaking:** • Creating a soap opera scene • Discussing good and bad manners	➤ **Reading:** *The Power of Poetry* ➤ **Writing:** • A scene from a soap opera • A haiku (poem)	➤ Learning styles and preferences
➤ **Listening:** • Unusual punishments • Good advice ➤ **Speaking:** • Choosing an appropriate punishment • Describing a life-changing experience	➤ **Reading:** • An article about a robbery • *Points of View* ➤ **Writing:** Describing a life-changing experience	➤ Linking: Consonants
➤ **Listening:** • A laughter club • Jokes • Song – "When You're Smiling" ➤ **Speaking:** • Discussing how lifestyle affects health • Telling jokes	➤ **Reading:** • *Musicians on Call* • *Why Do We Laugh?* ➤ **Writing:** Learning English outside the classroom	➤ English outside the classroom

1 From me to you

✔ Means of communication
✔ Review of present and past forms; tag questions

1 ▶ Speaking

Work with a partner. Find at least ten different means of communication in the picture.

Example   *The sign in the store window gives information about a sale.*

2 ▶ Vocabulary: Sounds

a **AUDIO** Listen. Number the sounds in the order you hear them. What do the sounds communicate?

___ a happy person **whistling**
___ a horn **honking**
___ a telephone **ringing**
___ an angry person **shouting**
_1_ a dog **barking**
___ a person **whispering**

___ a frightened person **screaming**
___ an alarm clock **beeping**
___ a happy person **humming**
___ people **cheering** at a ball game
___ people **clapping** in a theater

b What is the difference in each pair of words below?

1 honking and humming   2 clapping and cheering   3 whistling and whispering

c **AUDIO** Listen. Then work with a partner and describe the sounds you heard.

d Which of the sounds do you hear most often where you live?

3 Reading

a Work with a partner. Discuss the questions.

1 How many different ways can you think of to send a message to someone far away?
2 How did people communicate before there was mail service?

b Read the article quickly. Write where each type of message is or was used.

1 drums _____   3 runners   _____
2 horns _____   4 the Pony Express _____

IN TOUCH

In trying to find new ways of keeping in touch over long distances, many societies around the world have developed the same ideas. These often involve reducing a message to a visual or auditory code that the sender and the receiver can recognize. In both North America and Africa, for example, some people use drums to communicate. Others use smoke signals. Since the late 1800s, tapping the telegraph key has served a similar purpose.

People in places like mountains or jungles, where visual contact may be difficult, have found some unusual ways of keeping in touch using musical instruments. The alphorn, a carved wooden horn up to 20 feet long, has been used to communicate between alpine peaks in Switzerland for two thousand years. The Maya and, later, the Aztec of Mexico and Central America used horns made from conch shells to signal from one pyramid to another.

Many societies throughout history have used runners–human messengers on foot–to keep in touch. One of the most famous examples was the Greek runner who ran 25 miles from Marathon to Athens to announce victory over the Persians in 490 B.C. He ran so fast that he collapsed and died of exhaustion after delivering the news. The modern marathon footrace is named in his honor. In North America, many Native American tribes were famous for their runners, and the civilizations in Central and South

America also used messengers on foot. In Africa, Zulu runners were famous for their speed and endurance.

During North America's frontier days, the Pony Express was operated by a private company between April 1860 and October 1861. Horseback riders were posted at 157 stations over the 1,800 miles from Missouri to California. Changing horses six to eight times between stations, they carried letters from the East Coast to the West Coast in about ten days.

c Read the article again. Work with a partner. Answer the questions in your own words.

1 What do drums, smoke signals, and the telegraph have in common?
2 Why are horns useful in mountains and jungles?
3 Where does the word *marathon* come from?
4 How did the Pony Express work?

d Find words and expressions in the article that relate to communication.

e Name three ways that communication has changed in your lifetime.

Focus on Grammar

a Look at the sentences in the chart.

1 Find the following:

> **be** as an auxiliary verb   a verb in the simple present   a verb in the simple past
> an *-ing* form   a past participle

2 How do you form the continuous? How do you form the passive?

Review of present and past forms		
	Present	*Past*
Simple	Some people **use** drums to communicate.	The Greeks **used** runners to carry messages.
Continuous	I**'m using** the computer right now.	People **were** still **using** horses in 1860.
Passive	Alphorns **are used** in Switzerland.	The Pony Express **was used** during the frontier days.

Note:
- Continuous forms describe an action that is ongoing, in progress, or changing.
- Use the passive when the emphasis is on the process or action (not on the person or thing).
- Use *do* and *did* to form questions and negatives with simple tenses.

b Choose the simple or continuous form.

1 (I try / (I'm trying)) to call my aunt in Hong Kong, but I can't get through.
2 E-mail messages (usually arrive / are usually arriving) in seconds.
3 The World Wide Web is enormous—and it (still grows / is still growing).
4 My boss (uses / is using) the computer right now, so I (write / am writing) this letter by hand.
5 I (called / was calling) you at 6:00 last night, but you weren't home. (Did you get / Were you getting) my message?
6 The radio (played / was playing) so loudly that I couldn't hear a thing.

c Complete the paragraph with the active or passive of the simple present or simple past of the verbs in parentheses.

Many people ¹____*raise*____ (raise) carrier pigeons as a hobby, but the birds ² __*are rarely used*__ (rarely use) nowadays as a system of communication. However, the police department of the state of Orissa, in eastern India, ³_____ (operate) a carrier pigeon service until 2002. The carrier pigeon, or p-mail, as it ⁴_____ (call), ⁵_____ (provide) daily communications between 400 police stations in this remote area. In 1999, pigeons ⁶_____ (use) extensively during a cyclone. Today, the police stations ⁷_____ (link) by telecommunications.

d Work with a partner. Name a means of communication for each item.

> something was invented recently   something that's getting more and more popular
> something that was more popular ten years ago   something not used any more

5 ▶ Speaking

a Work in small groups. Discuss which types of communication you could use for each situation (1–6).

letter	fax message	e-mail message	face-to-face conversation
text message	voicemail	card	telephone conversation

1 You want to invite some friends to dinner at your house.
2 You recently stayed at a hotel where the service was very bad. You want to complain.
3 You would like to apologize to a colleague for something that happened at work.
4 You want to ask someone for a job.
5 You will be visiting a city where old friends live. You want to ask if you can stay with them.
6 You want to send a birthday greeting to someone in another country.

b Discuss the questions.

1 When you have something difficult to communicate, do you generally prefer to write it or to say it?
2 What kinds of things should probably not be discussed in e-mail?
3 Which means of communication do you find most useful?

6 ▶ Writing

a Look at the types of communication in 5a. Choose the means of communication you use most and least often. Make notes under the headings.

Means of communication you use most often:	When and why do you use it?	Means of communication you use least often:	Why don't you use it?

b Use your notes to write one paragraph on each topic.

c Work with a partner. Read each other's paragraphs. How similar or different are your answers?

Listening

a Work with a partner. Discuss the questions.

1 What is gossip?
2 Does everybody gossip?
3 Why do you think people like to gossip?

b **AUDIO** Listen to the interview with a sociologist. How does she answer the questions above?

c **AUDIO** Listen again. Write T (true) or F (false).

1 Most gossip is negative. ___
2 Gossip is about ourselves as well as other people. ___
3 A lot of informal conversation is gossip. ___
4 Men talk about other people more than about themselves. ___
5 Gossip helps us to feel part of a community. ___
6 Thanks to modern communications, we can now gossip more than ever. ___

d Who do you gossip with most often? What do you gossip about?

In Conversation

AUDIO What are these people planning to do? Listen. Then read.

Celia: Guess what? We're planning a party for Margie. She's getting married next month.
James: Really? I didn't know that.
Celia: Well, she didn't tell anyone. It's incredible, isn't it?
James: Wow! Yes. Where's the party going to be?
Berta: Well, we were thinking… we could have it in a restaurant, couldn't we?
James: Good idea.
Celia: What about *Paulo's* on Broad Street? You've been there, haven't you? We had Sasha's party there.
Berta: Oh, yes. I know it. It's a good place.
Celia: You won't say anything to Margie, will you? It's a surprise.
James: No…don't worry. I won't say a word.

9 ▶ Focus on Grammar

a Match the beginnings (1–4) with the tags (a–d). How do you form tag questions in the simple present and simple past?

1 You're not afraid, ___   a didn't he?
2 It was a good movie, ___   b don't you?
3 You have a car, ___   c are you?
4 Tom got a new job, ___   d wasn't it?

b Now look at the chart. How do you form tag questions with *have* and modals?

Tag questions: *have* and modals
Have
You**'ve been** there, **haven't you?**
James **hasn't heard** about it, **has he?**
Modals
We **could have** it in a restaurant, **couldn't we?**
He **should go** to the party, **shouldn't he?**
You **won't talk** to Margie, **will you?**

▼ Help Desk

Remember that the *'s* contraction can be *has* or *is*.

She's working. (= is)

She's gone. (= has)

c Write the endings of the tag questions.

1 They can do it, *can't they*?
2 You don't have a cell phone, _____?
3 You won't be late, _____?
4 Barbara's written a book, _____?
5 Kevin works pretty hard, _____?
6 We shouldn't tell Margie, _____?
7 We've met before, _____?
8 You would help me, _____?

10 ▶ *KnowHow*: Intonation with tag questions

a **AUDIO** Listen and repeat the tag questions. Notice the falling intonation—the voice goes down at the end. (The speaker expects the listener to agree.)

It's cold outside, isn't it?
You haven't been here before, have you?
You'll let me know, won't you?

b **AUDIO** Now listen and repeat the same questions with rising intonation—the voice goes up at the end. (The speaker isn't sure of the answer.)

c Complete the questions. Then ask a partner. Use rising or falling intonation depending on how sure you are of the answer.

The weather's ___ today, isn't it?   You live in ___, don't you?
You haven't ___, have you?   You don't like ___, do you?

Continue a conversation on one of the topics. Then switch partners.

11 ▶ Vocabulary: Expressions with *have*

a Look at the types of expressions that are used with *have*. Match a sentence with each category.

1 Do you have an appointment?   <u>1f</u>
2 Our neighbors have a new car.   __
3 Let's have a cup of coffee.   __
4 My sister's sick. She has the flu.   __
5 I have long dark hair.   __
6 They have two daughters and   __
a son.

have	a possessions
	b family
	c illnesses
	d meals and food
	e appearance
	f events (meetings, interviews, etc.)

b Work with a partner. Respond to each question or statement using an expression with *have*.

1 A: Why are you wearing a suit? (an interview)   B: *I have an interview this morning.*
2 A: We're going away this weekend. (a good time)   B: _____
3 A: Is Rose a grandmother already? (two grandchildren)   B: _____
4 A: We're hungry. (dinner)   B: _____
5 A: Are Mike's parents very rich? (money)   B: _____
6 A: Why is your mother in the hospital? (operation)   B: _____
7 A: Why didn't you write that letter? (time)   B: _____
8 A: Why is the neighbor's house noisy tonight? (party)   B: _____

12 ▶ Listening

a Look at the picture. Do you think Terry and Vince are talking about work?

b **AUDIO** Listen to the conversation. Match the people they are talking about with the topics.

1 Abby   __   a a dinner party
2 Josh   __   b a broken ankle
3 Elaine   __   c a new job

c **AUDIO** Listen again. Choose the correct ending.

1 Terry doesn't feel well because __.
a she has a cold   b she has an interview   c she has a meeting

2 Abby is upset because __.
a she broke her leg   b she can't go to work   c she can't run in the marathon

3 Josh starts his new job __.
a this week   b next week   c next month

4 Josh is going to take the bus to work because __.
a it's cheap   b it's direct   c he doesn't have a car

5 Vince is going to have a party __.
a at 8:00   b on Sunday   c on Saturday

13 ▶ Language in Action: Conversation strategies

a **AUDIO** Listen to the conversation in section 12 again. Check the expressions that you hear.

NEW INFORMATION	CHANGING THE SUBJECT	ASKING SOMEONE TO WAIT	ENDING THE CONVERSATION
__ Did you hear about…!	__ By the way,…	__ Let me see.	__ Anyway,…
__ Guess what! (informal)	__ Before I forget,…	__ Just a minute.	__ I have to go.
	__ That reminds me,…	__ Hold on / Hang on a minute. (informal)	__ That's about it.

b Complete the conversation with expressions from the chart. (More than one answer is sometimes possible.)

A: ¹_____! I'm having a party. It's on Sunday afternoon.

B: That sounds great.

A: I've invited Miriam and George.

B: Oh, good. ²_____, do you have George's number? I want to ask him something.

A: Sure. ³_____. It's 441-9076.

B: Thanks.

A: You're welcome. ⁴_____. I'll see you on Sunday.

c Role-play a telephone conversation. Use the prompts below.

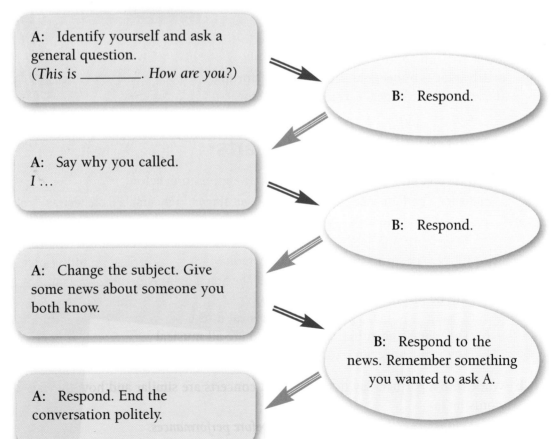

A: Identify yourself and ask a general question.
(*This is _____. How are you?*)

B: Respond.

A: Say why you called.
I …

B: Respond.

A: Change the subject. Give some news about someone you both know.

B: Respond to the news. Remember something you wanted to ask A.

A: Respond. End the conversation politely.

2 *In the limelight*

✔ Artists and authors
✔ Present perfect continuous; questions with prepositions

1 Listening

Track 10

a Look at the pictures. Have you ever performed in public?

b **AUDIO** Listen to the interview with Erin Neff, a professional singer. Put the topics in the order you hear her talk about them.

    __ free time
    _1_ her work
    __ how she started
    __ how she feels before a performance

c **AUDIO** Listen again. What does Erin say about …

    1 playing boys' roles
    2 her voice teacher
    3 getting nervous
    4 her schedule
    5 her social life
    6 the accordion

d What are some of the advantages and disadvantages of being a professional performer (for example, a singer, a dancer, or an actor)?

2 Vocabulary: The performing arts

a Fill in the blanks with one of the words or expressions below.

audience performance instruments lead singer rehearsals orchestras role scene stage

1 Actors perform on a(n) _____*stage*_____ in front of a(n) _____.
2 Actors and musicians have many _____ before they perform in public.
3 Juliet appears on the balcony in a famous _____ in the play *Romeo and Juliet*.
4 In tonight's _____ of *The Sound of Music*, the _____ of Maria will be played by Amelia O'Connor.
5 _____ often play classical music.
6 The piano, the guitar, and the violin _____ .
7 The main singer in a rock band i_____ .

b Work with a partner. Say how plays an[d] _____ [ho]w they are different. Use the words in 2a.

    Example *They both have rehearsals b[efore]*

3 Focus on Grammar

a Look at the sentences in the chart. Choose the correct answer.

1 The present perfect (simple / continuous) emphasizes an action in progress.
2 The present perfect (simple / continuous) emphasizes achievement or results.

Present perfect continuous and present perfect simple	
Present perfect continuous (*have + been + -ing*)	*Present perfect simple* (*have* + past participle)
I**'ve been singing** professionally for seven years. We**'ve been working** on *The Magic Flute*. Erin **has been learning** to play the accordion.	I**'ve had** several boys' roles. We**'ve done** that opera before. She **hasn't learned** very much yet.
Note: With some verbs like *live* and *work* the present perfect simple and present perfect continuous often have a similar meaning. *He's been working here for four years.* OR *He's worked here for four years.*	

b Circle the correct form.

1 I'm sorry I haven't (written / been writing) you a letter before now. I've (worked / been working) very hard.
2 Have you (heard / been hearing) the news? Marcus has (won / been winning) the music competition!
3 I know that opera well. I've (seen / been seeing) it several times.
4 I've (thought / been thinking) about taking piano lessons since I stopped working, but I haven't (taken / been taking) a class yet.
5 Bill has (painted / been painting) the living room all weekend, but he still hasn't (finished / been finishing).

c Work with a partner. Ask and answer questions about the people in the chart.

Example A: *What does Erin do?*
B: *She sings opera.*
A: *How long has she been doing that?*
B: *For about seven years.*
A: *How many different operas has she been in?*
B: *About fifty.*

Person	What?	How long?	How many?
Erin	sings opera	seven years	be in / 50 operas
Michael	writes poetry	since he was a teenager	write / 2 books of poems
Amber	paints	since she was 18	sell / about 20 paintings
Eddie	plays in a rock band	since he graduated	play in / a lot of concerts

d Work with a partner. Talk about yourself or someone you know who has an interesting hobby or talent.

4 ▷ Reading

a Which words describe the kind of music you like?

romantic sad fast-paced traditional classical popular loud rock

b Read the article about Prince Ndedi Eyango. Write the number of the paragraph that gives information about…

1 performance and tours. __
2 language and lyrics. __
3 his life and career. __
4 his style of music. __

PRINCE Eyango

Cameroonian singer and songwriter Prince Ndedi Eyango isn't concerned if his audience doesn't understand the lyrics in his songs, written mainly in his native tongues of Douala and Bamileke. "I always tell people this music doesn't need a language," he says. "It's all based on melody, harmony, and rhythm. I was dancing like crazy and humming the melodies when I heard American pop songs on the radio as a kid," he recalls. "I didn't understand a word, but I loved them anyway."

Eyango plays "makossa"—a type of folk music associated with the city of Douala in Cameroon. But his music is more fast-paced, and his style is his own. He uses electric instruments, and his music has elements of rhythm and blues, funk, and reggae as well as more traditional influences.

Eyango grew up in small villages in Cameroon, but later moved to France. He planned to study music in Paris, but within a year, he got a recording contract. He recorded his first five albums in Paris before moving to Los Angeles in 1993. In Los Angeles, he has continued making recordings, including the acclaimed CD "Si tu me mens" ("If you lie to me").

Prince Eyango tours regularly throughout Europe, Africa, Canada, and the U.S., and he has appeared at many international jazz festivals.

c Explain each of these words or expressions, and say why they are mentioned in the text.

1 Douala and Bamileke   2 makossa   3 "Si tu me mens"

d Make a list of words in the article that are related to music.

e Is it important for you to understand the lyrics in order to enjoy a song? Why or why not?

5 ▶ Speaking and Writing

a Think of a musician that you like. Make notes under the headings.

Name	Style of music	Life and career	Current activities

b Work in small groups. Use the notes to give a short presentation about the musician. Say why you like his or her music. Answer questions about the musician.

c Write a short article about the musician. Include information your group asked about.

d Work with a partner from a different group. Read each other's articles. Ask two questions about your partner's musician.

6 ▶ Language in Action: Compromises

a AUDIO Listen. Who is going to sing, Mario or Rena?

b AUDIO Listen again and fill in the blanks. Check your answers with the chart below.

Track 11

Larry: OK, let's have some music.
      ¹ *Can anybody* sing a song?
Rudy: Not me. I can't sing.
Janice: Mario can. Mario,
      ² _____ sing a song?
Mario: Oh, no. Honestly I'm not…
Larry: Oh, ³ _____, Mario!
Mario: ⁴ _____ really
      _____.
Janice: OK. Rena, what about you? Can you sing something?
Rudy: Yes! Come on, Rena! You ⁵ _____!
Rena: Well, OK, ⁶ _____ you all join in.

PERSUADING	REFUSING POLITELY	COMPROMISING
Can anybody…?	(Honestly,) I can't.	Well, OK, as long as…
Why don't you…?	(I'm sorry,) I'd really rather not.	All right, if you insist.
(Oh,) come on! (informal)		
You can do it!		

c Work in small groups. Find one thing that each person can do. Try to persuade someone to perform for the group. (If you don't want to perform, refuse politely.) Use the expressions in the chart.

    Example *Can anybody (sing a song / draw a picture / say a poem / dance)?*

7 ▶ Reading

HW

a Work with a partner. Discuss the questions.

1 Do you generally like science fiction books and movies? Why or why not?

2 What do you think a writer does to prepare to write a science fiction novel?

b Read the article about Michael Crichton quickly. Check the topics that are mentioned.

1 The reasons for Crichton's success   __

2 His childhood   __

3 The research he does for his books   __

4 His process of writing   __

5 His friends and social life   __

6 How he feels about success   __

Michael Crichton was born in Chicago, Illinois, in 1942. After graduating from Harvard medical school, he began a career as a writer and filmmaker.

THE Writing Life

Michael Crichton has written thirteen novels in the past 30 years. He has also written an award-winning TV show and the screenplays for several popular movies, including the blockbuster *Jurassic Park*. His books are sometimes criticized by scientists and book reviewers for not being "serious" enough, but his ability to blend the suspense of a thriller with the technical emphasis of science fiction has made him a favorite with readers around the world.

Crichton has been producing best sellers for 30 years–since he was a dissatisfied medical student at Harvard–and selling them to movie studios for enormous sums. But he is at heart a perpetual student. Most of his novels begin with an interest in a topic, which soon turns into a mountain of books. "I start to think more and more about a particular subject, and I can't let go," he says. "Usually I'm not sure why." His current interests are volcanoes, hot-air balloons, comets, the kingdom of Bhutan, the life of Leonardo da Vinci, the American Revolution, the behavior of plants, and child development.

The technical aspect of his writing also requires an enormous amount of research. For the novel *Timeline*, set in medieval Europe, Crichton read more than 200 books. Even after he began writing, there would be annoying little facts that he did not have. Each item of food, each building material had to be true to the period.

Crichton says the process of writing is not easy for him. He writes seven days a week in a room with little furniture to minimize distractions. For the duration of each book, he eats the same thing for lunch every day and allows himself little interruption except for exercise and family. As the writing progresses, he wakes up earlier and earlier each day, until he is at the computer at 2:00 a.m.

Despite all his success and good fortune, Crichton is quite modest. He claims he has no idea why his books and movies are so popular and says that he simply follows his own interests in writing them. He says it is "kind of bizarre" how his life has turned out.

c Read the article again. Say whether you think Michael Crichton would <u>agree</u> or <u>disagree</u> with each statement. Give reasons from the text for your answers.

> Example   Scientific or historical accuracy in novels is not important. All readers care about is a good story. *I think he would disagree. The article describes how much research he does for his books.*

1 It is possible to learn a lot about many different subjects from writing.
2 It is important to take vacations and days off, even when writing.
3 Writing requires absolute concentration.
4 To be successful, you must choose a topic for a book based on what readers will find interesting, not your personal interests.

d What do you think of Crichton's lifestyle?

8 ▶ Vocabulary: Research

a Match the words (1–7) with the definitions (a–g). (All of the words are in the article on page 13.)

1	behavior	<u>1d</u>	a	a part of a situation, idea, or problem
2	subject	___	b	a series of actions that you do for a particular purpose
3	development	___	c	pieces of information
4	aspect	___	d	how someone or something acts
5	research	___	e	the change in someone or something over time
6	facts	___	f	an area of knowledge, such as history
7	process	___	g	work that involves finding out about a subject

b Using the words above, say what you would have to do in each of the following situations.

gathering information for a biography   **choosing a school to attend**   **investigating a crime**

9 ▶ Speaking

a Choose an activity that you do (for example, studying, playing an instrument or a sport) or a hobby that you have. Think about the answers to the questions below.

1 Do you have to do any preparation before you begin? If so, what?
2 Do you have anything special that you do, wear, or use to help you?
3 What time of day is best for you to do it?
4 How often do you have to do it to be successful?
5 Is it better to do it alone or with other people?
6 Do you do the activity in a special place?
7 What makes you feel that you have been successful at the activity?

b Use your answers from above to describe your working process to a partner. How similar or different is the working process for each of you?

10 ▶ Listening

Track 12 **a** What usually happens on TV games shows?

b <u>AUDIO</u> Listen to part of a game show. Say three things that you learned about the contestant.

Track 13 **c** <u>AUDIO</u> Now listen to the next part of the show. As you listen, circle the answer that you think is correct in each case. Then see if you are correct.

1	a Spain	b Kenya		c Italy	
2	a hydrogen and oxygen	b hydrogen and calcium		c oxygen and nitrogen	
3	a keep on	b kick over		c knock out	
4	a observing planets	b measuring land movements		c regulating temperature	

d <u>AUDIO</u> Listen again. Can you write the four questions that were asked?

11 ▶ Focus on Grammar

a Look at the chart. Where is the preposition in each question?

Questions with prepositions	
Statements	*Questions*
Michael Crichton is famous for his novels.	What is Michael Crichton famous **for**?
Risotto comes from Italy.	Where does risotto come **from**?
Erin has been in many operas.	How many operas has Erin been **in**?

b Make questions for the missing information. Then ask a partner the questions. Which ones can you answer?

1 Princess Diana was married to _____.   *Who was Princess Diana married to?*
2 Cheese is made from _____.   _____
3 The letters VCR stand for _____.   _____
4 The Boy Scout movement was founded by _____.   _____
5 The movie *Jurassic Park* is about _____.   _____
6 The game of baseball originally came from _____.   _____

c <u>AUDIO</u> Listen and check your answers.

d Work with a partner. Complete the sentences about yourself. Then ask and answer questions about each other.

Example A: *What are you interested in?*   B: *Cooking, folk music, and photography.*

1 I'm interested in _____.
2 I'd like to learn about _____.
3 I'm pretty good at _____.
4 I enjoy talking to _____ about _____.
5 I usually agree with _____.
6 I've never thought about _____.

12 ▶ Speaking

a Imagine these are topics for a TV game show. Which topics would you choose to answer questions about? Number the topics in order of preference. (1 = first choice)

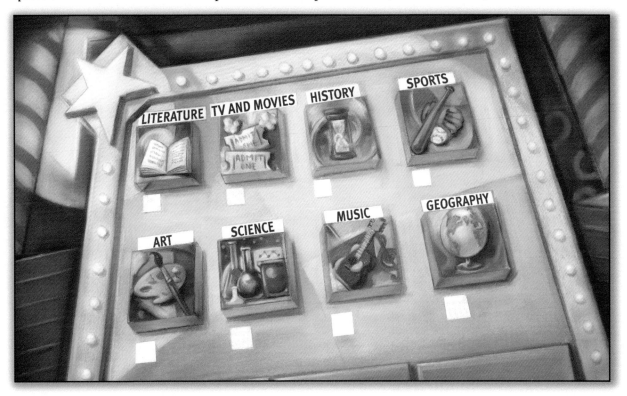

b Find someone who has chosen the same first or second topic. Write four questions about the topic. (You must know the answers.)

c Work in small groups. Take turns asking the questions. How many people can answer them?

13 ▶ *KnowHow*: Priorities in learning English

a Check all the things you have to do or would like to do better in English.

___ speak English when making friends from other countries
___ speak English at work
___ understand movies, TV, or music in English
___ read newspapers or magazines in English
___ read English for work or school (for example, business reports or textbooks)
___ write informal correspondence in English (for example, e-mails or letters)
___ write reports or academic papers in English
___ pass exams in English
___ other: _____

b Work in small groups. Compare your choices. Which of the following areas are most important to you?

speaking   listening   reading   writing   grammar   vocabulary

c Think of three things you can do in class to achieve your goals.

3 By coincidence

✔ Coincidences and connections
✔ Past perfect; relative clauses (object)

1 ▶ Listening

Track # 15

a Look at the pictures. How might these items be connected in a story?

b **AUDIO** Listen to *Table for Two* (part 1). Say how the pictures are related to the story. Were your guesses correct?

c **AUDIO** Listen again. Check the <u>three</u> false statements.

1   The speaker is the daughter of Deborah and Joseph. ___
2   Deborah was studying art history. ___
3   Deborah went to the restaurant to meet someone. ___
4   Joseph sat at her table because the restaurant was crowded. ___
5   Joseph and Deborah liked each other immediately. ___
6   Deborah gave Joseph a piece of paper. ___

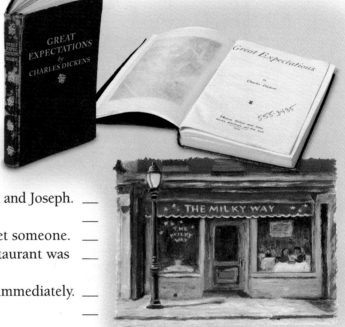

d Work with a partner. Discuss two possible endings for the story.

2 ▶ Vocabulary: Phrasal verbs

Read this summary of Charles Dickens's *Great Expectations*. Then choose the correct meaning for the phrasal verbs below (1–8).

Pip is a poor orphan without a great future. His parents have **passed away**, and he is being **brought up** by his sister and her husband, who do not treat him well. At the beginning of the book, Pip **runs into** a mysterious stranger and helps him. Pip is frightened by the event, but he forgets about it when he meets the wealthy Miss Havisham, and her adopted daughter, Estella. Estella is beautiful, and Pip soon **falls for** her. Eventually, Pip **comes into** a lot of money and lives the life of a rich man. He believes that the money comes from Miss Havisham. But then the stranger, Magwitch, **turns up** again unexpectedly and tells Pip the truth. It **turns out** that Pip's money has come from Magwitch all along, and that Magwitch is Estella's father! When Pip hears this, he asks Estella to marry him. She isn't interested, and she **turns him down**…

1	pass away:	(a die)	b	become successful
2	bring (someone) up:	a teach	b	raise
3	run into (someone):	a fight with	b	meet by accident
4	fall for (someone):	a help	b	fall in love with
5	come into (money):	a receive	b	lose
6	turn up:	a appear	b	leave
7	turn out:	a believe	b	happen in the end
8	turn (someone) down:	a accept	b	reject

3 ▶ Reading

a Fill in the blanks with the details of the story that you remember from section 1. (Use the pictures on page 17 to help you).

b Now read the rest of the story. How did Deborah and Joseph meet the second time?

The story so far:

The writer's parents, Deborah and Joseph, first met at ¹_____ in New York. Deborah was sitting alone reading ²_____ . Joseph sat at her table because the restaurant was crowded. They started a conversation, and got along very well. At the end of the evening, Deborah gave Joseph the book with ³_____ written in it.

The next day, my father traveled out to Brooklyn to visit his parents. He brought the book to read on the subway, but he was exhausted after his sleepless night. So he slipped the book into the pocket of his coat—which he had put on the seat next to him—and closed his eyes. He didn't wake until the train reached the far side of Brooklyn.

When my father opened his eyes and reached for his things, the coat was no longer there. Someone had stolen it, and because the book was in the pocket, the book was gone, too. And so my mother's telephone number was also gone. In his excitement over meeting Deborah, he had forgotten to ask her last name. The telephone number was his only link to her.

The call that my mother was expecting never came. My father looked for her several times at the university, but he could never find her.

That summer, they both headed for Europe. My mother went to England to take literature courses, and my father went to Paris. During a three-day break in her studies, my mother flew to Paris, determined to see as much as she could in 72 hours. She carried a new copy of *Great Expectations* on the trip. She had not had the heart to read it, but now, as she sat down in a crowded restaurant after a long day of sight-seeing, she opened it to the first page and started thinking about Joseph again.

She was interrupted by a waiter who asked her, first in French, then in English, if she could share her table. She agreed and then returned to her reading. A moment later, she heard his voice.

"A tragic life for poor dear Pip," the voice said. Then she looked up, and there he was again.

c Read the story again. Put the events in order.

___ Joseph saw Deborah again.
___ Joseph looked for Deborah at the university.
_1_ Joseph got on the train.
___ Deborah went to a restaurant in Paris.
___ Joseph fell asleep on the train.
___ Deborah went to England.
___ Deborah went to Paris.
___ Joseph's coat was stolen.
___ Joseph put the book in his pocket.

d How did Joseph and Deborah feel about each other? Find words and expressions in the story that support your opinion.

4 ▶ Focus on Grammar

a Look at the chart and respond to items 1 and 2 below.

1 The past perfect is used to show that something happened (a long time ago / earlier than something else).

2 How do you form the past perfect?

Past perfect	
Simple past	*Past perfect*
Joseph **put** the book into his coat, which	he **had put** on the seat next to him
He **fell** asleep because	he **hadn't slept** the night before.
When Joseph **woke** up, he realized that	someone **had stolen** the coat.
Questions	*Answers*
Had Deborah **been** to Europe before?	Yes, she had. / No, she hadn't.
Finally Deborah came home. Where **had** she **been**?	She didn't say.

b Complete the paragraph with the simple past or past perfect tense of the verb in parentheses.

Last week, I ¹_____*went*_____ (go) to dinner at a friend's house. I ²_____ (meet) a man from India who ³_____ (spend) many years in the United States as a young man. We ⁴_____ (talk) about the places where he ⁵_____ (be). He ⁶_____ (travel) extensively, so he ⁷_____ (know) a lot about the country. As he was speaking, I ⁸_____ (have) a strange feeling that I ⁹_____ (meet) him before.

5 ▶ Vocabulary: Time expressions

a Look at the expressions that describe when events happen. Find two examples on page 18.

the day **before** (that) the **previous** day	the **same** day **that** day	the **next** day the day **after** (that) the **following** day	**two** days **later**

Note: Instead of *day*, you can also use words like *morning, afternoon, night, week, month,* or *year.*
the next night, two years later

b Use the itinerary to complete the sentences with time expressions. Sometimes more than one answer is possible.

1 We took a cruise around Sydney Harbor on July 17. _____*That night*_____, we went to bed early! We were tired because we had arrived in Sydney late _____.

2 _____, we visited the Blue Mountains, and _____, we had dinner in a seafood restaurant.

3 _____, we went shopping. We left Sydney _____ and flew to Melbourne.

July 16
Evening: Arrived in Sydney.

July 17
All day: Took a cruise around Sydney Harbor. Went to bed early!

July 18
Morning: Visited the Blue Mountains
Evening: Had dinner at a wonderful seafood restaurant.

July 19
Morning: Went shopping near the hotel.
Evening: Flew to Melbourne.

6 Listening

a Look at the picture. How long do you think Franco and Benedetto have known each other?

b [AUDIO] Listen to Franco's son tell a story about the men. Choose the most appropriate title.

    a   An Unfortunate Tractor Accident
    b   A Hard Life in Sicily
    c   Old Friends Meet Again
    d   Searching for a Friend for Forty-nine Years

Franco Balistreri and Benedetto Ingallina

c [AUDIO] Listen again. Answer the questions.

1   Where are Franco and Benedetto originally from?   _Sicily, Italy_
2   How old was Franco when he went to work on the farm?   _____
3   Who did Franco and his brother meet at the farm?   _2 other brothers_
4   How was Franco injured?   _tractor_
5   How long was Franco in the hospital?   _6 months_
6   Where did Franco and Benedetto meet the second time?   _NY   wedding_
7   How long have they been living in the same neighborhood?   _~~28~~ 49 yrs_

d Work with a partner. Discuss how the two men's lives have been similar. Then describe what happened the last time you ran into an old friend.

7 Speaking and Writing

a Think of a story about a coincidence or an unusual event that happened to you or to someone you know. Answer the questions. Make notes.

1   When did it happen? Where were you and what were you doing?
2   What happened first? What happened after that? What did you do / say / feel?
3   How did the event affect you afterward?

> ▼ **Help Desk**
>
> *happen* = take place
>
> That **happened** a long time ago.
>
> *happen* + *to* + verb = do something by chance
>
> They **happened to live** in the same neighborhood.

b Work with a partner. **A**, tell your story. **B**, listen to your partner's story. Ask questions about it. Then switch roles.

c Work with a new partner. Tell your story again, adding the details that your first partner asked about.

d Write your story. Try to write at least one page. Include more details to make it interesting.

8 ▶ Reading

a What does the expression *It's a small world* mean? When would you use it?

b Read the article quickly to find the answers to the following questions.

1 What is the "small world phenomenon"?
2 What did Milgram discover in his experiment?
3 What are researchers doing now?

> **▼ Help Desk**
>
> Don't confuse *experience* and *experiment*.
>
> an *experience* = something that has happened to you
>
> an *experiment* = a scientific test to prove something

Six Degrees of S·e·p·a·r·a·t·i·o·n?

Have you ever heard something from a friend of a friend? Or thought you knew somebody who knew somebody who knew the president? Stanley Milgram believed that such chains were the world's basic social communication system.

Milgram was a Harvard University social psychologist and father of the "small world phenomenon": the theory that everybody is connected to everybody else by short chains of social acquaintances. (1)

In 1967, Milgram sent 300 letters to randomly 2 selected addresses in Omaha, Nebraska and Wichita, Kansas. Each letter contained a small packet and instructions to get the packet to a person in the Boston area that was known as the target. The letter provided the target's name, location, and occupation.

The Nebraskans and Kansans could only send the packet to the target through a chain of personal contacts—people they knew on a first-name basis. Those people were also supposed to send it along using the same criteria—through people they knew such as friends of friends, relatives, or business connections, getting closer and closer to the target each time.

Sixty packets, through sixty different chains of people, eventually reached the target. Of those, Milgram found that the average number of people in the chain was about six, a discovery that was called the "six degrees of separation." Milgram theorized that we are only a short chain away from anyone else and that the implications of such a small world could be enormous in business and communications.

Now researchers at Columbia University are testing Milgram's hypothesis for the entire world. Using e-mail, they are trying to determine whether everyone is indeed only six social acquaintances away from everyone else.

They may find that, because of rapid communication, the world is even smaller than it used to be, or that we've grown farther apart and have fewer acquaintances to build chains with.

c Read the article again. Find a word or expression in the article that means the same as items 1–6. (2) = paragraph number.

1 people you know (2)   *social acquaintances*
2 not in any special order (3)   _____
3 knowing someone well enough to use his or her first name (4) _____
4 standards (4)   _____
5 possible effects (of a theory) (5)   _____
6 a theory (6)   _____

d Work with a partner. Describe Milgram's experiment. Use expressions from 8c.

e What do you think the Columbia University researchers will find out?

9 ▶ Speaking

a Work with a partner. Imagine you have to try to send a package to one of these people through someone you know on a first-name basis. Say which person you would try to contact and how you might be able to reach him or her.

b Compare your ideas in small groups. Based on your results, do you agree with Milgram's theory? Why or why not?

A nurse in Jamaica

A journalist in Spain

An English student in Vietnam

A software developer in the United States

10 ▶ Focus on Grammar

a Look at the chart. What words can be left out of these relative clauses?

Relative clauses (object)		
Who is Diana?	Diana is someone	**that / who I met at a party.**
	Diana is someone	**I met at a party.**
What's that?	It's the letter	**that / which we were waiting for.**
	It's the letter	**we were waiting for.**

Note: Remember that the relative pronoun cannot be left out when it is the **subject** of the relative clause. I know someone **that / who knows the president** (Not: ~~I know someone knows the president.~~)

b Cross out *that* and *who* when possible.

When I visited the town ~~that~~ I grew up in, I met a man ~~that~~ I had gone to school with. He was living on the same street that his parents lived on and was married to a woman who taught in the high school. We had a long chat about the good times that we had as children and the people that we used to know. One of the people that I asked about was Kathy Gilhooley, the daughter of the man that owned the largest department store in town. "Oh, she's the woman who I married!" he replied.

c Work with a partner. Give an example for each item.

Example   *John is a person that I work with.*

a person you work with   a person you get along well with   a person you look like
something you're afraid of   something you're looking forward to

Language in Action: Confirmation

a   **AUDIO** Listen to the introductions. What do the people ask about in each case? Are they correct, partially correct, or incorrect? Make notes in the chart.

17

work in gov't

Person / Place	Question	Correct	Partially correct	Incorrect
1 Marco Freitas	*Politician?*		✓	
2 Kyoto, Japan		✓		
3 Raisa				✓

b   **AUDIO** Listen again. Check the expressions that you hear.

IDENTIFYING	CONFIRMING	APOLOGIZING
__ Are you the (person) that...? __ Is that the (person) that...? __ Is that (the place) where...? __ That's..., isn't it?	__ (Yes.) That's right. __ Exactly. **CORRECTING** __ Not exactly. (Actually, ...) __ I'm not really.... (In fact, ...)	__ Oh yes, that's right. __ I'd forgotten. __ I got the names mixed up.

c   Work in groups of three. Take turns introducing each other. Continue the conversations as in the example. Keep on talking!

Example   A: *I'd like you to meet…. He / She lives in / works at / studies….*
          B: *Oh! Are you the (person) that…?*
          C: *That's right / Not exactly. Actually, I….*

KnowHow: Contrastive stress

a   **AUDIO** Listen to this conversation. B stresses *you*, but A doesn't. Why? A stresses *on*, but B doesn't. Why?

18

A: Oh, you're from Australia. What part of Australia are you from?
B: I'm from Sydney. What about you?
A: I'm from Porto Alegre, Brazil.
B: Where is Porto Alegre? Is it in on the coast?
A: Well, it's not exactly on the coast, but it's near the coast.

b   **AUDIO** Read this conversation. Mark the words that you think are stressed. Then listen and check your answers.

19

A: Do you work in Vancouver?
B: I don't, but my wife does. She's a nurse at the hospital. What about you?
A: I'm a nurse too, but I'm at a clinic.
B: Really? The one on Green Street?
A: No, the one on Pine Street.

c   Practice both conversations in this section.

13 Listening: Song

a AUDIO Look at the picture. Then cover the words and listen. What is the song about?

b AUDIO Read the song. Try to fill in the blanks with these words. Then listen and check your answers.

20

bought	grows	ice	mine	romance	same
say	shine	stared	started	umbrella	waiting

Bus Stop

Bus stop, wet day, she's there, I ¹ _say_
Please share my umbrella
Bus stop, bus goes, she stays, love ² _____
Under my umbrella

All that summer we enjoyed it
Wind and rain and ³ _____
That umbrella we employed it
By August, she was ⁴ _____

Every morning I would see her
   ⁵ _____ at the stop
Sometimes she'd shop and she would show
   me what she'd ⁶ _____
Other people ⁷ _stared_
   as if we were both quite insane
Someday my name and hers
   are going to be the ⁸ _same_

That's the way the whole thing ⁹ _started_
Silly, but it's true
Thinking of a sweet ¹⁰ _romance_
Beginning in a queue

Came the sun the ¹¹ _ice_ was melting
No more sheltering now
Nice to think that that ¹² _umbrella_
Led me to a vow

> **queue** = people waiting in line.

c Imagine you are one of the people in the song, a few years later. Tell a partner how you met.

d Do you know any people who met in an unusual way? Describe how they met.

24

Units 1–3 Review

Grammar

1 Read the article. What do people like about the Art Studio? What does Phil find exciting about the work?

THE ART STUDIO
Phil Sylvester founded the Art Studio, where he teaches people to draw and paint, in 1991. He had become an architect several years before and had taught drawing in a design school. Phil now teaches about 70 people a week. "Almost everybody who comes to the studio knows somebody who has had classes here. People like the supportive atmosphere, so they tell others about it," he says. "Art gives people the chance to learn about themselves and discover what they are able to do. They constantly amaze me, and themselves, which is what's so exciting about doing this."

2 Complete the conversation with the verbs in parentheses. Choose from the tenses indicated in each section.

Simple present or simple past:

Alain: What ¹ _do you do_ (you / do), Phil?
Phil: I ² __am__ (be) a drawing teacher. I also ³ _paint_ (paint), and I ⁴ _make_ (make) unusual guitars.
Alain: Really? How ⁵ __did__ (you / get) into that?

Simple past or past progressive:

Phil: A friend and I ⁷ _talked_ (talk) about how to make a guitar last year. He ⁸ _gave_ (give) me the

parts to make a guitar. I ⁹ _played_ (play) around with the stuff for hours one day when I ¹⁰ _realized_ (realize) that I could make guitars that are also works of art.

Past or present (active or passive):

Alain: ¹¹ __Did__ (you / make) that guitar over there?
Phil: No, that one ¹² _was made_ (make) by a famous Spanish guitar maker. It's pretty old. In fact, they say it ¹³_was played_(play) by Segovia. I sometimes ¹⁴ __use__ (use) it as a model for a new instrument.
Alain: It's beautiful. What kind of wood ¹⁵ _is it made_ (it / make) of?
Phil: Well, it's made of…

3 Complete the tag questions.

1 Tae hasn't painted in years, _has he_?
2 You won't give up playing in the band, _will you_?
3 He can make friends really easily, _can't he_?
4 Jenny should buy one of your guitars, _shouldn't she_?
5 You've seen her dance, _haven't you_?
6 He couldn't be a professional singer, _could he_?

4 Complete the conversation with the correct form of the present perfect or present perfect continuous.

A: What ¹ _have you been doing_ (you / do) lately, Lydia?
B: ² _have been_ (I / plan) a tour for my dance company.
A: Really? ³ _Have you_ (you / go) _gone_ on a tour before?
B: No, not really. ⁴ _have performed_ (we / perform) in a few nearby towns, but ⁵ _we haven't gone_ (we / not go) to other countries before. ⁶ _I have almost_ (I / almost finish) making the arrangements, though, and I'm really excited!

25

5 Write the verbs in parentheses in the simple past or past perfect. Each sentence has one of each.

I ¹ _had known_ (know) Karl for several years before I ² _realized_ (realize) that we were related. We ³ _had not talked_ (not talk) about our families before, but one day we ⁴ _started_ (start) comparing our backgrounds. It ⁵ _turned out_ (turn out) that his great-grandfather ⁶ _had come_ (come) to Brazil just a few months before my great-grandmother and her sisters. Karl's great-grandfather ⁷ _had known_ (know) my great-aunt Enid for only a few weeks before they ⁸ _decided_ (decide) to get married.

6 Combine the sentences. Use relative clauses.

1 Lydia is a dancer. Andrew met her in Peru. _Lydia is the dancer who/that Andrew met in Peru. (OR...the dancer Andrew met in Peru.)_

2 And these are the paintings. He bought them in a gallery in Lima. _____

_____

3 Andrew gave me a painting. I asked him for it. _____

_____

4 The painting is next to the photos. We took them last summer. _____

_____

Vocabulary

7 Fill in the blanks with the appropriate form of the phrasal verbs.

bring up	run into	turn out
come into	turn down	fall for

1 Edwin was _brought up_ by his grandparents because his parents had died.
2 She had a lot of trouble with the painting, but it _turned out_ exactly as she had planned.

3 Marissa will _come into_ a lot of money when she turns twenty-five.
4 I _ran into_ Petra while I was shopping. I hadn't seen her for a long time.
5 You won't _turn down_ the job if they offer it to you, will you?
6 Women always _fall for_ him because he is good-looking and intelligent.

Recycling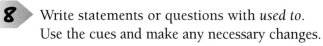

8 Write statements or questions with _used to_. Use the cues and make any necessary changes.

1 Phil teaches at the "Studio" now. (a design school) _Phil used to teach at a design school_.
2 Sophie writes novels now. (poetry)
_____.

3 Letters to California travel by airmail. (Pony Express)
_____.

4 Do you send messages by e-mail? (telegraph) _____.
5 Does Liz record on CDs now? (cassettes) _____.

Fun Spot

ANAGRAMS

Use the letters of the underlined word(s) to form another word (or words). Each sentence contains a clue with the meaning of the new word.

Example _Go pine_ for a messenger bird.
Answer _pigeon (a bird used as a messenger)_

1 This means of communication is a <u>great help</u>.
— — — — — — — — —

2 They <u>share real</u> music after much practice.
— — — — — — — — —

3 The <u>gates</u> lead to a performance area.
— — — — —

4 These fire messages are <u>making losses</u>.
— — — — —   — — — — — — —

4 A day's work

✔ Jobs and work experience
✔ Gerunds and infinitives; *it* + infinitive

1 ▶ Listening

a Work with a partner. Look at the occupations in the pictures. Discuss the questions.

1 What does each person do?
2 What question would you ask each person about his or her job?

2 Alex, stock trader

4 Ed, tollbooth worker

jail

1 Ryan, pizza chef

3 Nigel, costume designer

5 Melissa, salesperson

b **AUDIO** Listen to the people talking about the questions they are often asked about their jobs. Write one question that each person is asked.

1 Ryan _Are you sick of pizza?_ *Sure*
2 Alex _Wall street   invest   accounting I work in acc'ing_
3 Nigel _movies, famous movie stars → very nice_
4 Ed _boring   BRoom   I don't mind working for 8 hrs_
5 Melissa _____ *discount 30%*_

> ### ▼ Help Desk
>
> *Work* is an uncountable noun.
> *I'm looking for* **work**.
> *Job* is a countable noun.
> *I got* **a job** *in a hotel.*

c **AUDIO** Listen again. Note the answer(s) that each person gives.

d What would you ask each of these people about their job?

a TV weather reporter   a pilot   a mail carrier   a bus driver   a detective

2 ▶ Focus on Grammar

a Choose the correct form of the verb in parentheses in the sentences. Then look at the chart. What category would you put *don't mind, want,* and *enjoy* in (verb + gerund OR verb + infinitive)?

> I don't mind (working / to work) as a pizza chef. But when I want (order / to order) out, I get something else. I enjoy (eating / to eat) different kinds of food.

Gerunds and infinitives	
Verb + gerund (-ing)	
You **get used to working** with famous people. People **keep asking** me if I'm sick of pizza.	*keep, stop, suggest, can't help, look forward to, be / get used to*
Verb + infinitive (to + base form)	
Most people **seem to think** my job is really boring. People ask me why I **decided to do** it.	*seem, decide, promise, offer, refuse*
Note: These verbs can be followed by a gerund or an infinitive with no real change in meaning: *begin, start, continue, prefer.* Stop can also be followed by an infinitive of purpose. *We stopped* (in order) *to have a cup of coffee.*	

b Complete the paragraph with the correct forms of the verbs below. Some verbs may be used more than once.

> apply   feel   hire   give   work   get

Alex wanted to work as a journalist, so he decided <u>¹ to apply</u> for jobs with newspapers. He contacted the local paper, but they refused ²_____ him because he didn't have experience. A second editor promised ³_____ him an interview but then said she had stopped ⁴_____ new employees. Alex couldn't help ⁵_____ disappointed. Finally, someone suggested ⁶_____ without pay to get some experience. So Alex offered ⁷_____ at a local radio station. The manager liked him and decided ⁸_____ him a job with pay. He's really looking forward to ⁹_____ his first paycheck.

c Finish these sentences with your own information. Use a gerund or an infinitive.

1 I'm not used to _____.
2 I've decided _____.
3 I'm looking forward to _____.
4 I've stopped _____.

> **▼ Help Desk**
>
> *Be / get used to* means to be or become accustomed to something.
>
> *I'm used to starting work early.* (It's normal for me.)

3 ▶ *KnowHow*: Dictionary tips / Verbs

a Use a dictionary to find out about verbs. Look at the verbs in the dictionary extract and answer the questions.

1 What information is given about each verb?
2 Which verbs are followed by a gerund?
3 Which verb is followed by an infinitive?

b Add the verbs to the chart in 2a. Then write a sentence using each verb.

> **risk** /rɪsk/ *verb* [T] to take the chance that sth bad could happen: *If you don't study hard now, you risk failing your final exams.*
> **involve** /ɪnˈvɑlv/ *verb* [T] to make necessary: *The job involves traveling.*
> **pretend** /prɪˈtɛnd/ *verb* [I,T] to appear to do or be sth, in order to trick or deceive sb: *Paul's not really asleep. He's just pretending. The kids are pretending to be astronauts.*

4 ▶ Vocabulary: Nouns functioning as adjectives

a Look at the job titles. Note how the nouns *software*, *U.S.*, and *marketing* function as adjectives to modify other nouns.

> *A software designer* = a **designer** of **software**
> *The U.S. marketing director* = the **director** of **marketing** for **the U.S.**

b Write job titles for these people. (Hint: Work in reverse order!)

1 a **representative** in charge of **service** to the **customer**   *a customer service representative*
2 a **manager** of a **project**   _____
3 a **technician** at a **laboratory**   _____
4 an **owner** of a **restaurant**   _____
5 a **designer** of **graphics** for the **computer**   _____
6 a **clerk** who works at a **desk** in a **hotel**   _____

c Work with a partner. Discuss what you think these people do.

food production supervisor   **recording studio engineer**   **car insurance salesperson**

5 ▶ Language in Action: Saying you're not sure

a **AUDIO** Listen and complete the conversation. Then check your answers with the chart below.

Paul: What does Stephanie do?
Justin: I'm not sure exactly. She [1] *has something to do with* computers.
Paul: Does she work in sales?
Justin: No, I think she's [2] _____ consultant. She goes to companies, sets up their computer systems, and [3] _____.
Paul: Oh, I see. She's a systems analyst.
Justin: Well, [4] _____ anyway.

JOBS	WORK ACTIVITIES	
She has **something to do with** (computers).		**and that kind of thing.**
She's **a kind of** (consultant).	She (sets up computer systems)	**and things like that.**
She's a (consultant) or **something like that.**		**and so on.**

b Practice the conversation above, using alternative expressions from the chart where possible.

c Work with a partner. Talk about people you know.

> Example   **A:** *My friend (name) works in…. He / She's a kind of….*
> **B:** *What exactly does he / she do?*
> **A:** *I'm not sure. I think he / she…, and that kind of thing.*

6 ▶ Writing

a Read the paragraphs. What kind of jobs are these people describing? Are they describing positive or negative aspects?

One of the unpleasant aspects of Paul's job is the irregular schedule. Sometimes programmers have to work really late to finish a project or to meet a deadline. That can be a problem for people because it affects their personal and social lives.

The best part of my job is feeling that I'm helping people. Most patients are very grateful to the nurses and doctors who take care of them. It feels good to know that I am making a difference in people's lives, especially when I see people get better and go home.

b Think of a job that you know well. Make notes under the headings.

Job Title: _____	
Positive aspects	***Negative aspects***

c You have been asked to write a paragraph about the job for possible job candidates. Use your notes and the examples in 6a to help you.

d Work with a partner. Exchange papers. Ask some questions about the job your partner has written about.

7 ▶ Speaking

a Decide and check (✓) the three features that would be most important for you in a job.
__ good benefits (for example, paid vacation or sick time)
__ a good salary
__ being able to balance your personal life with your career
__ opportunities to travel
__ opportunities to learn
__ helpful and / or inspiring colleagues
__ a well-known employer
__ job security
__ variety of assignments

b Work in small groups. Compare your answers. Give reasons for your choices.

8 ▶ Listening

a What jobs do you know that involve hardship or danger?
What do you think about them?

2^B

b **AUDIO** Listen to the introduction to a TV program. Choose the correct summary.

New View magazine

___ Many people would like to have these kinds of jobs.

___ The jobs are exciting, but they're not popular.

___ The jobs have very good working conditions.

c **AUDIO** Now listen to the interviews. Answer the questions.

1 What do / did the people like about their jobs?
Michael (roofer): *outdoors   meet people*
Phil (seaman): *crazy   leader action excitement*
Connie (cowgirl): *lots of satisfaction seasonal free time*

2 Which person has stopped working? _____
sea man

d **AUDIO** Listen to the interviews again. Who says each of the following? Write M, P, or C.
(M = Michael, P = Phil, C = Connie)

1 "I like being outdoors." ___
2 "I can't imagine doing anything else." ___
3 "I don't regret doing it for a moment." ___
4 "I enjoy working in different places." ___
5 "No one tells you what to do." ___
6 "Would I do it again? Yes!" ___

9 ▶ In Conversation

AUDIO What point is Dr. Moya making? Listen. Then read.

Host: Welcome to the show, Dr. Moya.

Dr. Moya: Thank you. It's nice to be here.

Host: Tell me… What do you think of the *New View* report about the worst jobs?

Dr. Moya: Well, I think it's wrong to talk about "the worst jobs" or "the best jobs." A job that's good for one person can be a disaster for someone else.

Host: I notice that a lot of people like to have some freedom in their job—to be able to set their own working hours, for example.

Dr. Moya: Yes, that's right. But for others it's important to have security. The thing is, it's impossible to generalize.

ON AIR

10 ▶ Focus on Grammar

a Look at the sentences in the chart. Then find two more examples of *it…* + infinitive in the conversation on page 31.

It… + infinitive		
It's + adjective It's a good idea It takes time / costs money	+ infinitive	**It's nice to be** here. **It's important to have** security. **It's a good idea to find out** about the job. **It takes time to learn** a profession.

b Rewrite these sentences. Begin each sentence with *it.*

1 Becoming a doctor takes a long time.   *It takes a long time to become a doctor.*
2 Asking people about their salary isn't polite.   *It isn't polite* _____
3 Hiring new staff costs a lot of money.   *It costs* _____
4 Traveling is necessary in this job.   *It's* _____
5 Working at home is sometimes a good idea.   _____
6 Having a job that you like is important.   _____

c Work with a partner. Finish the sentences, using an expression with *it.*

When you're having an interview…   **If you're applying for a job…**   **In your first job…**

11 ▶ Vocabulary: Expressions with *set, keep, meet, raise*

Look at the diagrams. Then complete the memo with the correct forms of the verbs.

set	a deadline, a goal a clock, a watch a date, a time your own hours

keep	a journal, a record a promise, a secret quiet, still cool, warm

meet	a deadline, a goal (someone) for lunch famous people

raise	prices, salaries money for charity children

MEETING MINUTES ....

- The meeting started at 11:00. Frank gave a presentation on the Levine project. We ¹ _set_ a new deadline to finish the project. If we want to ² _meet_ that deadline, we may need to hire more staff.

- Sayuri gave us some information about the salary adjustments. Management expects to ³ _keep_ its promise to ⁴ _raise_ all salaries by 5% this year.

- Office managers will ⁵ _meet_ for lunch next week in the fourth floor cafeteria. At that meeting they will ⁶ _set_ a date for the charity walk. We hope to ⁷ _raise_ $3,500 for charity. Let's try to ⁸ _meet_ that goal!

Reading

a Read the caption about Frank McCourt. What do you learn about him?

b You are going to read an extract from *'Tis*, in which McCourt describes one of his first jobs as a temporary office worker, or "temp," in New York City. What kind of work do you think a "temp" does?

c Read the extract. What happens at the end?

Frank McCourt grew up in Limerick, Ireland, and he moved to America in 1949. His autobiography, *Angela's Ashes*, made him famous. In *'Tis*, the second part of his autobiography, McCourt describes his early years in New York.

FRANK McCOURT 'TIS

They send me to offices all over Manhattan. From nine to five I sit at desks and type lists, invoices, addresses on envelopes, bills of lading. Supervisors tell me what to do and talk to me only when I make mistakes. The other office workers ignore me because I'm only temporary, a temp they say, and I might not even be here tomorrow. They don't even see me. I could die at my desk and they'd talk past me about what they saw on TV last night and how they're getting outa here fast Friday afternoon. They send out for coffee and pastries and don't ask me if I have a mouth in my head. Whenever anything unusual happens, it's an excuse for a party. I'm not invited to the parties and I feel strange with my typewriter clacking away and everyone having a good time.

I don't know how they can work in these offices day after day, year in, year out. I can't stop looking at the clock and there are times I think I'll just get up and walk away the way I did at the insurance company. The people in their offices don't seem to mind. They go to the water cooler, they go to the toilet, they walk from desk to desk and chat, they call from desk to desk on the telephone, they admire each other's clothes, hair, makeup and anytime someone loses a few pounds on a diet. Office people brag about their children, their wives, their husbands and they dream about the two week vacation.

I'm sent to an import-export firm on Fourth Avenue. I'm given a pile of papers that have to do with importing Japanese dolls. I'm supposed to copy this paper to that paper. It's 9:30 a.m. by the office clock. I look out the window. The sun is shining. A man and a woman are kissing outside a coffee shop across the avenue. It's 9:33 a.m. by the office clock. The man and woman separate and walk in opposite directions. They turn. They run toward each other to kiss again. It's 9:36 a.m. by the office clock. I take my jacket from the back of the chair and slip it on. The office manager stands at his cubicle door and says, Hey, what's up? I don't answer. People are waiting for the elevator but I head for the stairs and run as fast as I can down seven flights.

d Read the extract again. Answer the questions.

1 What kind of work does Frank have to do?
2 What do the other office workers do?
3 What happens when they have parties?
4 Why do you think Frank leaves the office?

e Write T (true), F (false), or NI (no information). Refer to page 33 to justify your answers.

1 Frank only works in one office. ___
2 He feels part of a team. ___
3 He frequently talks to the other office workers. ___
4 He has never left a job before. ___
5 Time passes slowly in the job. ___
6 Frank is not going to go back to the office. ___

f What would you do in Frank's situation?

13 ▶ Speaking

a Look at the cartoons. Explain the meaning of each one. Which one do you like best?

1

"Well, being single and a robot, I'm able to put in a lot of overtime."

3

"Keep up the good work, whatever it is, whoever you are."

2

4

"Honey, are you thinking about the office?"

b Each cartoon highlights a workplace problem in a humorous way. Work in small groups. For each cartoon, decide what the "problem" is and what people could do about it.

Example Cartoon # 1   Problem: *Employers expect employees to work long hours.*
Solution: *Reduce work hours / hire more people…*

5 The nature of things

✔ Ecology and natural phenomena
✔ Passive forms; time clauses

1 ▶ Reading

a Look at the picture. Why do you think the penguin is wearing a sweater?

b Read the article quickly and answer these questions.
1 What happened to the penguins?
2 Why did they need sweaters?
3 Why did so many sweaters arrive?

BEST-DRESSED PENGUINS ARE WEARING WOOL THIS YEAR

Animal lovers around the world have helped to save thousands of oil-soaked little penguins on Philip Island, in southern Australia–by knitting sweaters for them. Ten thousand penguin-sized wool sweaters have arrived at the offices of the Tasmanian Conservation Trust in response to their call for emergency insulation for a population of the world's smallest penguins.

The birds were endangered last year when an oil spill washed into their habitat. The oil covered the birds' waterproof feathers, preventing them from swimming to look for food. Conservation workers moved fast to save the birds from starvation, hypothermia, and oil poisoning. But they needed a way to keep the tiny penguins warm after they'd been caught and washed. Then workers thought of using wool sweaters. Tight-fitting woolens provide ideal protection for the birds because, like feathers, wool is an excellent insulator.

They published a knitting pattern for penguin sweaters in a free newspaper for elderly Australians. But when the story was picked up by BBC radio and broadcast all over the world, the penguins' problem became international. Sweaters started arriving from around the world, in all colors and fashions including local football team colors. Demand has now been met, and the small sweaters are being saved in case of future oil spills.

c Read the article again. Match the words (1–7) with the definitions (a–g). (1) = paragraph number.

1	knitting (1)	_1e_	a	dying from hunger
2	insulation (1)	___	b	a material that protects something from cold or heat
3	spill (2)	___	c	a design for making a piece of clothing
4	habitat (2)	___	d	liquid that has poured out by accident
5	waterproof (2)	___	e	making something (like a sweater) from wool
6	starvation (2)	___	f	not letting water through
7	pattern (3)	___	g	the natural home of a plant or an animal

d What do you think of this story? Do you know of any other situations where people helped animals in danger?

2 ▶ Focus on Grammar

a Look at the chart and complete the rules using the words below.

have   be   been   being

1 To form the passive with the present and past continuous, use a form of _be_ + _____ + the past participle.

2 To form the passive with the present and past perfect, use a form of _____ + _____ + the past participle.

Passive: Continuous and perfect forms	
Present continuous	**Present perfect**
The habitats **are being threatened** right now.	The penguins' problem **has** now **been solved**.
Past continuous	**Past perfect**
The penguins **were being threatened** by hypothermia.	Rescuers put sweaters on the penguins after they **had been caught** and **washed**.

b Fill in the missing words in the paragraph.

has   been (2x)   had   are   is

Mongolian horses are descended from the last truly wild horses on earth. But by the 1960s, all of Mongolia's original wild horses had *been* killed or domesticated. Many been caught in the early 1900s and brought to European zoos and farms. In the last ten years, several groups have tried to reintroduce wild horses to Mongolia. An area being set aside as a protected area for the horses. Several groups of horses have brought to Mongolia already and more animals being reintroduced to the country. Now, some 60 horses are living once again on the steppes of Mongolia, and the program been declared a success.

3 ▶ Vocabulary: Prefixes

a Prefixes such as *over-*, *re-*, and *mis-* can help you to understand new words. Look at the chart. Then use the prefixes to help you guess the meanings of the underlined words in the headlines.

Prefix	Meaning
re-	again
over-	too much
co-	with, together
mis-	wrongly or badly
de-	taking away from

WOLVES <u>REINTRODUCED</u> TO NATIONAL PARKS:
"We Must Learn to <u>Coexist</u>," Say Park Officials

ENVIRONMENTAL GROUP PROTESTS <u>DEFORESTATION</u> AND <u>OVERFISHING</u>

OFFICIAL ACCUSED OF <u>MISLEADING</u> INVESTIGATORS

CITY PLANS TO EXTEND DOWNTOWN AREA: RESIDENTS TO BE <u>RELOCATED</u>

b Work with a partner. Say what you think the stories in the headlines are about.

4 Listening

a Look at the picture and discuss the questions.

1 Why do people visit national parks? What can you do there?

2 How might tourism affect the environment in a park?

3 Look at the sign. What warning does it give?

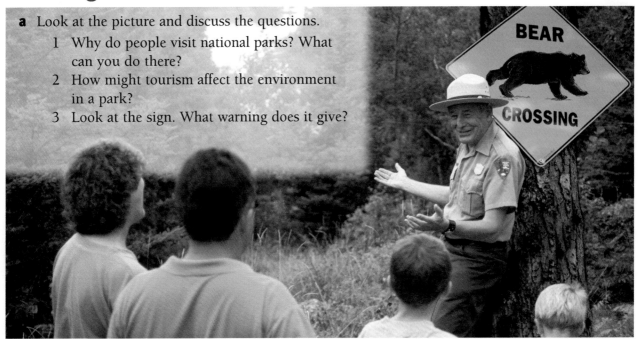

b **AUDIO** Listen to a park ranger talking to visitors at a national park. Which three of these topics does he mention?

traffic control   water pollution   camping   trash   bears

c **AUDIO** Listen again. Give at least one reason for each of the following situations.

1 The roads have been closed.

2 The park is quieter.

3 You have to make a reservation to camp in the park.

4 You have to keep food in locked containers.

5 Eating campers' food endangers wild animals.

d Would you like to visit a park like this? Why or why not?

5 Speaking and Writing

a Read the newspaper article. What is the problem?

b Imagine you are one of these people. Decide how you feel about the new road, and why. Then work in small groups. Try to convince others of your point of view.

the town mayor   a forest ranger   a tourist
a hotel owner   a construction worker

c What do you think the town should do? Write a letter to the newspaper giving your own opinion about this problem. Say what you think is the best solution and why. Begin like this:

Dear Editor:

I read the recent article about the proposed new road at Hightown. I think that…

HIGHTOWN: A growing controversy over a proposed new road has polarized the inhabitants of this small community in the mountains. Located at the entrance to the western rainforest, the town is popular with tourists as an entry point to the spectacular National Rainforest Preserve. The town is accessible only by a very rough, unpaved road. A recent proposal to improve the road has met with opposition from some of the local people, but is being welcomed by the town's mayor, who believes that

6 ▶ Language in Action: Advice and warnings

a **AUDIO** Some visitors are going canoeing at a national park. Listen to the guide. What does she tell the visitors to do?

b **AUDIO** Listen again. Complete the phrases in the chart with expressions from the conversation.

2

> **GIVING ADVICE AND WARNINGS**
> - Don't forget to ¹ *keep your life jackets on* .
> - ² *Take sunscreen with you,* in case ³ _____.
> - Make sure you ⁴ _____.
> - Watch out for ⁵ _____.
> - Be careful not to ⁶ _____.

> ▼ **Help Desk**
>
> *In case* indicates that something is possible.
>
> Take sunscreen with you **in case** it gets sunny.

Quiz 2

c Work with a partner. Imagine he or she is about to do one of the following activities. Have a conversation where you give some advice and warnings. Use expressions from the chart.

> go on a camping trip   take children to a beach / zoo / amusement park
> go to a big outdoor concert

7 ▶ *KnowHow*: Linking

a **AUDIO** Understanding how words are connected in spoken English helps you understand what you hear. Listen and repeat. Pay attention to how the words are linked together.

28

> **Consonant / vowel:**
> Watch out!
> Don't stand up in the boat.
> Do you have a jacket?
> Get it out and put it on!
>
> **Same consonants:**
> Take care. Don't forget to write.
> It's a cold day. Here's some hot tea.

b Read the poem aloud. Practice linking the words where indicated.

c **AUDIO** Listen and check your pronunciation.

29

> When rainy daylight fades away
> And dusk turns into night
> The cityscape, so gray by day,
> Becomes a maze of light.
>
> Along its streets the traffic curves
> And leaves behind a trace
> Of glistening colors—blue, red, white,
> Reflected in its face.
>
> The buildings soar like sparkling towers
> Above the city's sound
> And overlook a sea of lights
> Upon the glittering ground.

> **Glossary**
>
> **glistening, sparkling, glittering** = shining
>
> **maze** = a complicated pattern (of paths)
>
> **soar** = to be very tall

Vocabulary: Natural phenomena

Look at the map and the key. Then work with a partner and discuss the questions.

1 Which of the phenomena involve or produce…
   a movement of the earth?   b water?   c heat?   d snow?   e wind?
2 Which ones often happen at the same time?
3 Which ones are unusual where you live?

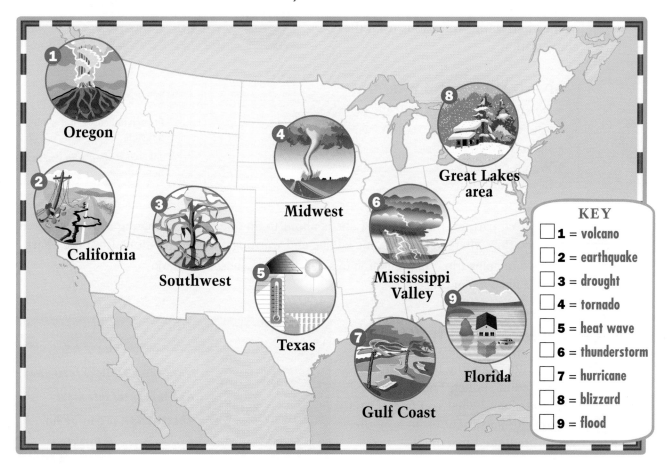

Oregon

California

Southwest

Texas

Midwest

Mississippi Valley

Gulf Coast

Great Lakes area

Florida

KEY
- [ ] **1** = volcano
- [ ] **2** = earthquake
- [ ] **3** = drought
- [ ] **4** = tornado
- [ ] **5** = heat wave
- [ ] **6** = thunderstorm
- [ ] **7** = hurricane
- [ ] **8** = blizzard
- [ ] **9** = flood

Listening

a Find these places on the map. Which phenomenon is shown for each place?

   the Great Lakes area   Texas   the Mississippi Valley   the Gulf Coast   Oregon   California

b AUDIO Listen to the news report. Check the events on the map key above that are mentioned.

c AUDIO Listen again and complete the chart.

cold air, north
record low temp

When?	Where?	What happened?	Result
January	Great Lakes area	blizzards	airports closed *20in. snow*
March	South and Southwest	*heat wave*	*100,000*
May	Mississippi Valley	*tornadoes*	*42 twisters*
September	*Gulf Coast*	*hurricane*	5,000 people were evacuated

high winds

d What is the weather like in a typical year where you live?

30
weather
record high temp

emergency shelter

airports closed   *wild fires*

In Conversation

AUDIO What should the students do if they hear a tornado warning? Listen. Then read.

Firefighter: OK, let's review the tornado drill. First, how will you know when a tornado is spotted in the area?

Student 1: There'll be a tornado warning.

Firefighter: That's right. You'll hear a siren. As soon as you hear the siren, move to the basement.

Student 2: Do we have to take anything with us?

Firefighter: No. You need to get to the basement as quickly as possible, and stay there until it's safe to leave. We'll let you know when the danger is over.

Focus on Grammar

a Look at the sentences in the chart. Then circle the correct answer for 1 and 2.

1 The sentences are about a possible event in the (past / present / future).

2 The time clause—in bold—is in a (past / present / future) form.

> **Time clauses (future)**
>
> **As soon as you hear the siren,** move to the basement.
> You should stay in the basement **until it's safe to leave.**
> We'll let you know **when the danger is over.**
> It'll be dark **by the time we get home.**
>
> ---
>
> **Note:** When a time clause begins a sentence, it is followed by a comma. Time clauses also begin with *before, after,* and *while.*

b Choose the correct expression.

1 Let's wait in the building (by the time / until) the rain stops.

2 We'll have a snack (while / before) we're waiting for the bus.

3 Check the weather forecast (as soon as / before) you go fishing.

4 I've sent you a postcard, but I'll probably be home (by the time / until) you get it.

5 We'll call you (as soon as / by the time) we hear any news.

c Finish these sentences with a subject and a verb. Use your own ideas.

1 I'm going to study English until _____.

2 As soon as I get home tonight, _____.

3 I'll be very tired by the time _____.

12 Reading

a Look at the pictures and the title of the article. What do you think this article is about? How do you think the town fought a volcano?

b Read the article quickly. Which paragraphs describe…

1 the first eruption? ___
2 the fight against the volcano? ___
3 the islanders' return? ___ and ___

The Town That Fought A VOLCANO... and Won

Fifteen islands make up Vestmannaeyjar, off the southern Iceland coast. Heimaey (pronounced hay-may) is the only one that is inhabited. Because of its superb natural harbor, it is Iceland's most important fishing port.

But on a cold January night in 1973, the fishing boats could not leave the harbor because of a fierce storm. As the island's 5,300 inhabitants slept peacefully, they had no idea that those boats would save their lives.

Suddenly, at about 2:00 a.m., the earth began to open up, slowly at first, until there was a fissure a mile wide less than half a mile from town. Boiling lava exploded 500 feet into the sky. Heimaey sat on top of a volcano nobody knew was there.

When they realized what was happening, the islanders ran for the fishing boats in the harbor. Within six hours, all 5,300 residents of the island were brought to the safety of the mainland.

The public applauded the rescue. But geologists began to worry. If the lava continued on its present track, it would fill the harbor. The harbor at Heimaey was responsible for a large proportion of Iceland's main export: fish.

It was then that they decided to spray the lava with seawater to make it change its course. Beginning with local fire trucks, then with fire boats, and finally with pumps borrowed from the U.S. Army, 500 people worked day and night for five months, spraying cold water on the lava. The conditions were so hot that their boots often caught fire. Burning rocks showered down on them from the still exploding volcano. Miraculously, no one was killed. And, even more miraculously, the lava stopped—one foot away from the harbor wall.

After the eruption was declared over, the islanders returned to an island that was 20% larger, had a more sheltered harbor, and two volcanoes instead of one. But many houses and buildings were lost forever under mountains of volcanic debris. Today, white signs mark where houses once stood.

Some of the people whose houses were buried in the lava never returned, unwilling to face the changed landscape of the island. But those who did return made an opportunity out of a disaster. They used the debris to improve the island's streets and lengthen the airport runway. For years after the eruption, the automatic system that watered the lava provided free heat for all the homes on Heimaey.

c Read the article again. Write questions for the answers. Sometimes more than one question is possible.

1 Because of its excellent harbor.
Why is Heimaey important? / Why is Heimaey Iceland's most important fishing port?

2 At about 2:00 a.m.
_____

3 They escaped on fishing boats.
_____

4 They thought that the lava would fill the harbor.
_____

5 By spraying seawater on the lava.
_____

6 No. It looked very different after the eruption.
_____

7 They used it to make the streets better.
_____

d Find these words in the article on page 41. Use the context to try to figure out what each word means. (1) = paragraph number.

inhabitants (2)   **fissure (3)**   **mainland (4)**   **spray (6)**   **debris (7)**

e Work with a partner. Discuss the questions.

1 How were the islanders lucky on the night of the eruption?
2 How did the eruption change the island?
3 How would you describe the people who lived on Heimaey?

13 ▶ Speaking

Work in small groups. Look at the photos. Discuss the questions.

1 Which of the places would you like / not like to live in? Why or why not?
2 What environmental feature would have the biggest effect on your life in each place?
3 How do you think people's characters are affected by the environment they live in?

6 Make your mark

✔ Heroes and fame
✔ *Could* and *be able to*; first and second conditionals

1 ► Listening

a Why do we admire certain people? What do you think might be admirable about the people in the pictures?

b **AUDIO** Listen to the people being described by others. Note one reason that each person or group is admirable.

c **AUDIO** Listen again. Answer the questions.

1 Why was it difficult for Wilma Rudolph to become an athlete?
2 Why did the woman dream about being Nancy Drew?
3 What do the coastguard volunteers say about what they do?
4 What did the man's father insist on?

d Which of the people do you find the most admirable?

1 Wilma Rudolph—Olympic runner

3 Volunteer Coastguard

2 Nancy Drew—Teenage detective

4 Arturo Salinas—Father

2 ► Vocabulary: Verbs and prepositions

a Fill in the blanks in the diagrams with *about, at, for,* or *on*.

b What is the difference between *look at* and *look for*?

c Complete the paragraph with prepositions.

Ethan was shy. He smiled ¹ *at* other children but rarely spoke. He concentrated hard ² ____ his school work. He read everything he could ³ ____ the natural world, and he dreamed ⁴ ____ a career as a scientist. He found out ⁵ ____ university programs, and applied ⁶ ____ a part-time job to help pay ⁷ ____ his education.

① smile wave stare look — *at* someone or something

③ apply look pay wait — ____ something

② dream learn read find out think — ____ someone or something

④ insist concentrate focus work — ____ something

3 ▶ Focus on Grammar

a Look at the sentences in the chart. What words and expressions are used to express ability…

   1 in the past?   2 in the present perfect?   3 in the future?

Ability: *could* and *be able to*	
Past (general ability)	Wilma Rudolph **could / was able to** run very fast.
Present perfect	The detectives **haven't been able to** solve the crime.
Future	If you work hard, you **will be able to** go to college.
Other forms	The doctors said Rudolph **would / might** never **be able to** walk.

Note: Use *could* for general ability in the past, but for a single event in the past, use *managed to*. *The coastguard managed to rescue the windsurfer.* (Not: ~~The coastguard could rescue the windsurfer.~~) *Couldn't* is used for both general ability and for a single event in the past.

b Insert the missing word in each sentence.

   to   be   been   able   weren't

   1 The coastguards looked for the swimmer, but they ʌ able to find him. *weren't*
   2 We won't be able tell you the results until Tuesday.
   3 My grandmother has never able to drive.
   4 Would you able to give me a ride home?
   5 If you ask the person over there, she might be to help you.

c Complete the paragraph with *could* or *managed to*.

After a long search, Lena ¹_____ find a job with a tailor. The tailor didn't believe that Lena ²_____ sew, but he changed his mind when he saw her work. When she started to work for him, he realized that she ³_____ work hard and that she ⁴_____ help him with the business, too. Lena eventually became his business partner, and together they ⁵_____ turn the small shop into a million-dollar business.

d Finish the sentences about yourself. Then compare your answers with a partner.

   I've never been able to…   I'd love to be able to…   One day, I'll be able to…

4 ▶ Speaking

a Think of someone that you admire: a public person or someone you know personally. Why do you admire him or her? Make notes in the chart.

Name: _____
Why I admire this person:
1
2
3

b Work with a partner. Describe the person you chose. Give details and examples of why you admire this person.

c Work in small groups. Decide which qualities you most admire in other people.

5 ▶ Reading

a Look at the pictures and discuss the questions.

1 What folk tales do the pictures remind you of?

2 What are some common characters and plots in folk tales?

3 Why do you think people have folk tales?

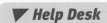

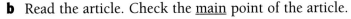

b Read the article. Check the <u>main</u> point of the article.

___ Folk tales can be serious or humorous.

___ Folk tales usually have a moral or a message about human behavior.

___ Folk tales everywhere have the same kinds of characters and plots.

People everywhere have stories of giants and witches, tricksters and fools, and people who turn into animals. What is remarkable is how similar these stories are from one culture to another. Most of the major themes recur in hundreds of versions from countries as far away from each other as India and Ireland. There are versions of the story *The Three Little Pigs* in several areas of the world.

The hero in many folk tales starts out as a lad, or the heroine as a young girl. Often he or she is powerless or disadvantaged in some way. Maybe the boy is the youngest of three brothers. Or the girl is a stepdaughter from a previous marriage in the lowest position in the family, like Cinderella. Usually the hero has to perform some "impossible" task. In one Russian tale, the hero must build a flying ship to go to the edge of the world; in another, a heroine must find a castle that lies east of the sun and west of the moon. At first it looks like they will never be able to complete the task. However, in the end they manage to succeed. In many stories, the hero or heroine receives help from a magical figure, often someone that he or she has helped by an act of kindness.

These stories contain a lesson to be learned. The happy ending of the tales shows that maturity and independence will come to those who have an honest and open attitude towards life and who help others.

Even the humorous stories have a moral. Trickster tales also have something serious to say—about the rights of the "little guy." In the Native American story *The Theft of Fire*, the trickster steals a spark of fire from a powerful and greedy old man, who is keeping all the fire for himself. Because we see that the trickster has right on his side, we identify with him even when he does not follow the letter of the law.

Almost every type of tale, no matter how trivial it may seem on the surface, has a message about human behavior. "Noodlehead" stories, for example, make us laugh at extreme cases of foolishness, but usually we ourselves are guilty of the same behavior in milder form. For example, in a popular tale from the Southern United States—*The Two Old Women's Bet*—a woman convinces her husband that he is wearing elegant clothes when he is not. We laugh at him, but we recognize how unwilling we are to trust our own senses when society tells us something different.

c Read the article again. Find an example in the article of…
   1 a story that exists in many different cultures.   *The Three Little Pigs*
   2 a disadvantaged heroine.   _____
   3 an impossible task.   _____
   4 a trickster story.   _____
   5 a "noodlehead" story.   _____

d Match the words on the left with definitions on the right. (1) = paragraph number.
   1 version (1)   <u>1g</u> a the place where a surface ends
   2 lad (2)   ___ b wanting more of something (food, money) than you need
   3 stepdaughter (2) ___ c a young boy
   4 edge (2)   ___ d being fully grown, developed, or adult
   5 maturity (3) ___ e the daughter of your wife or husband from an earlier marriage
   6 greedy (4)   ___ f unimportant
   7 trivial (5)   ___ g a story that is based on an original model, but has different details

e What kinds of heroes are shown in popular movies and TV programs?

6 ▶ Speaking and Writing

a Work in small groups. Choose a well-known folk tale and work together to tell it. Include as many details as you can remember.

b Write the tale by yourself. Try to write at least one page.

c Exchange stories with a partner from your group. How are your versions different?

d Look at your story again. Add three more details. Then rewrite your story.

e Read some tales written by people in other groups. Discuss the questions.
   1 Do any of the stories contain characters or plots similar to those described in the article?
   2 Do any of the stories contain a lesson to be learned? If so, what is it?

> **▼ Help Desk**
>
> Folk tales often begin like this:
>
> *Once upon a time,….*
>
> They sometimes end like this:
>
> *They lived happily ever after.*

7 ▸ Vocabulary: Suffixes

a Suffixes can indicate whether words are adjectives or nouns. Complete the chart with examples from the article on page 45.

Adjective suffixes		Noun suffixes	
-ate:	fortunate	-ism:	heroism
-ous:	previous, _____, _____	-ship:	friendship
-ish:	selfish	-ness:	kindness, _____
-y:	greedy, _____	-ity:	_____
-able / -ible:	_____, _____	-ence:	_____
-ful:	_____	-tion:	_____
-less:	_____	-ster:	_____
-al:	_____, _____, _____		

b Fill in the blanks with the correct form of the word in bold.

1 Jamaica is an **independent** nation. It achieved its _independence_ in 1962.
2 Seung is a great **friend**, and I really value her _____.
3 Teenagers think they're **mature**, but they often don't behave with _____.
4 Bob's sense of **humor** is usually great, but last night he told a joke that wasn't _____.
5 The mayor of the town has a lot of **power**. He's an extremely _____ man.

8 ▸ *KnowHow*: Using a dictionary / Word groups

a Use your dictionary to expand your vocabulary. Look at the dictionary extract below. Answer the questions.

1 What is unusual about the pronunciation of the *h* in *honest*?
2 Is *honest* used with people, things, or both?
3 How many different meanings are given for *honestly*?
4 What prefix is used to make the opposite of *honest* and *honesty*?
5 How many words are formed from the base word *honest*?

> **honest** /ˈɑnɪst/ *adj.* 1 (used about a person) telling the truth; not cheating or stealing: *Just be honest – do you like this skirt or not?* 2 showing honest qualities: *an honest face. I'd like your honest opinion.* The opposite for both senses is **dishonest.**
>
> **honestly** /ˈɑnɪstli/ *adv.* 1 in an honest way: *He tried to answer the lawyer's questions honestly.* 2 (used for emphasizing sth.) *I honestly don't know where she went.* 3 (used for expressing disapproval) *Honestly! What a mess!*
>
> **honesty** /ˈɑnəsti/ *noun* [U] the quality of being honest. The opposite is **dishonesty.**

b Look up these words in a dictionary. What other words are formed from them?

1 real   2 possible   3 fortune

c Write the new words from this page in your notebook. Group the words according to the base words. This will help you use them correctly.

9 ▶ Speaking

a Work with a partner. As fast as you can, write down the names of:

두 two well-known politicians
two famous actors or actresses
two famous singers or musicians
a TV personality
a sportsperson

b Work in small groups. Compare your lists. Why did you choose the people you did?

c Imagine your group is planning a dinner party. Choose six people from your lists to invite. Then present your plan to the class. Say why you chose each person.

10 ▶ Listening

a A recent poll asked people these two questions. How would you answer them?

1 It has been said that in the future, everyone will be famous for at least fifteen minutes. Do you think this is likely to happen to you?
2 If you were famous, how would you use your fame?

b **AUDIO** Listen to the news report and circle the correct answer—a, b, or c.

1 According to the poll, _b_ of Americans believe that they are likely to become famous.
   a 13%   b 30%   c 43%
2 A majority of people said they would __, if they were famous.
   a make themselves or their business better known
   b get a better job   c help people who are less fortunate
3 __ of the people interviewed believe(s) that he / she is (are) likely to be famous.
   a One   b Two   c Three

c **AUDIO** Listen to the interviews from the news report again. Complete the sentences.

Person 1: If she were famous, she wouldn't _____ give interviews
Person 2: If he became famous, he'd like to _____ help other.
Person 3: If she is successful, she'll _____ got a recording contract
                        musician   play music full-time

d How would you answer the questions in the survey?

Focus on Grammar

a Look at the sentences. Which person—A or B—feels he or she is more likely to become famous? How do you know?

A: "If I were famous, I'd hate it!"

B: "If I become famous, you'll be able to sell my autograph."

b Look at the chart. Fill in the blanks in items 1 and 2 with the words below.

a future form   a present form   a past form   would

1 To describe possible or likely situations, use _____ in the main clause and _____ in the *if* clause.

2 To describe hypothetical or imaginary situations, use _____ in the main clause and _____ in the *if* clause.

First and second conditionals: *if* and *unless*

First conditional (possible or likely situations)

If I **become** famous, you**'ll be able** to sell my autograph.
What **will** you do **if** you**'re** successful?
He **won't go** to the party **unless** someone famous **is** there.

Second conditional (hypothetical or imaginary situations)

If I **were** famous, I**'d hate** it!
If you **became** famous, how **would** you **use** your fame?
It **would be** hard to help people **unless** I **had** a lot of money.

Note: *Unless* means *if not* or *except if.*

---

c Complete the paragraphs with the correct form.

Group E in this year's World Cup consists of Brazil, Belgium, Nigeria, and Germany. Brazil and Germany [1] _will probably win_ (probably win) because they are both strong teams. If Brazil [2]_____ (win), the team [3]_____ (play) France in the next round. If Germany [4]_____ (win), they [5]_____ (go) against Ireland. I think Brazil and Germany [6]_____ (probably be) in the quarter-finals unless something very unusual [7]_____ (happen).
If I could put together my own team, I [8]_____ (choose) Roberto Bianconi of Italy. And if Nigel Smith of England [9]_____ (be) available, I [10]_____ (take) him, too. I [11]_____ (put) Paul Lamarre of France in the goal. He [12]_____ (not let) anything go past him.

d **AUDIO** Listen and check your answers.

e Choose the most logical word according to your situation and then finish the sentence. Then work with a partner and discuss your answers.

1 If [*name of a famous person*] (comes / came) to dinner, _____.

2 If our team (wins / won) the World Cup, _____.

3 If it (snows / snowed) tomorrow, _____.

4 I (won't / wouldn't) move to a different city unless _____.

12 ► Language in Action: Likelihood

a AUDIO Listen and complete the conversation.
Then check your answers with the chart below.

Gary: So what do you think?
1 _what the chances_ Naomi Lindberg
will get the best actress award?

Nina: 2 _Not a chance_! Not against
Jessica Murray.

Beth: Oh, I don't know. I'd say it's
3 _likely_. She gave a
fantastic performance in that movie.

Gary: I agree. Jessica Murray got it last year.
4 _I bet_ they'll give it to
Naomi Lindberg.

Nina: I guess they might.
5 _You never know_!

QUESTIONS		
Do you think (that)….		
What are the chances (that)…?		
How likely is it that…?		
ANSWERS: **LIKELY**	**LESS LIKELY**	**NOT LIKELY**
I bet… I expect (that)… It's likely (that)…	There's a chance (that)… You never know!	Not a chance! The chances are pretty small. It's unlikely (that)… I doubt (that)…

b Think of three questions about something in the future.
Write them down. Here are some things you can ask about:

a celebrity	an event in the news	a sporting event
a character in a TV show	the weather	a politician

Example *What are the chances that our team will win the game tonight?*

c Work with a partner. Ask one of your questions. Continue the conversation as in the example.

Example   A: *What are the chances that our team will win the game tonight?*
B: *I think it's very likely.*
A: *Why do you think so?*
B: *Well, because they've been playing very well, and they're a good team.*
A: *What will you do if they win?*
B: *I'll celebrate!*

d Do the same thing with your other questions. Ask different partners. Which predictions do you all agree on?

Units 4–6 Review

Grammar

1 Read the sign. What is an avalanche? What should you do if you are caught in one?

AVALANCHE FACTS–SKIERS BE CAREFUL!

• An avalanche is a natural phenomenon in which a large amount of snow slides down a mountain.
• Avalanches may happen after it has rained and then snowed, or when the weather is cold and then warms up suddenly.
• Avalanches are often set off by a small earthquake or by a person stepping in the wrong place.
• If you are caught in an avalanche, you should try to ride it like a surfer. Unless you keep your head above the snow, it will be very hard to get it out again.
• You should always ski or climb mountains in groups.
• Always carry a cell phone or radio in case you get lost.

2 Fill in the blanks with the verbs from the list. Use the gerund or infinitive form.

climb apply search help prepare practice

1 A group of skiers offered _to help_ with the rescue.
2 If you keep _____, you will become a good skier.

3 They decided _____ the mountain in the morning.
4 Thomas suggested _____ for a job with the mountain rescue team.
5 They stopped _____ for the lost skiers when it got dark.
6 It's necessary _____ carefully for such a difficult climb.

3 Rewrite the sentences in the passive.

1 They have fired several people from the Mountain Rescue team.
   Several people have been fired from the Mountain Rescue team.
2 They are discussing more budget cuts.
   _____
3 They are canceling the program.
   _____
4 They have mismanaged the budget.
   _____

4 Match the parts of the sentences.

1 It may be too late by the time   _1c_
2 As soon as we get to the airport,   __
3 We'll take some warm clothes in case   __
4 They haven't been able   __
5 Will you check the doors and windows before   __
6 Brenda and Jack could   __
7 While you're organizing the office,   __
8 I'll call a meeting after   __

a the weather changes.
b you leave the house?
c the rescuers get there.
d everyone is back in the office.
e run a mile in five minutes.
f we will give you a call.
g to find the missing papers.
h I'll buy some office supplies.

5 ▶ Complete the sentences. Use your own ideas.

1 I will get a good job if _____ _____.

2 If I were ever in Italy, _____ _____.

3 I would lose a lot of money if _____ _____.

4 I'll buy some extra food in case _____ _____.

5 If there is a tornado we, _____ _____.

Vocabulary

6 ▶ Fill in the blanks with the words below.

set   meet   stay   stare   focus

1 Can we __*set*__ a date now for the next meeting?

2 Can you _____ me for lunch at 1:00 on Friday?

3 You're welcome to _____ with us while you're in Buenos Aires.

4 You need to _____ on your work.

5 I hate it when people _____ at me.

7 ▶ Fill in the correct form of the word in parentheses. Add prefixes or suffixes.

1 This product was a success before, so they are planning to *reintroduce* (introduce) it.

2 Is it _____ (fool) or _____ (hero) that makes him do such dangerous things?

3 An-Li can be _____ (self) at times, but she is full of _____ (kind) when anyone is in trouble.

4 Sam gives most of his money to charity. It is _____ (remark) that such a wealthy person is not _____ (greed).

5 Because of _____ (forestation), wild animals are being forced to go into the cities and must _____ (exist) with humans.

Recycling Center

8 ▶ Fill in the correct tenses of the verbs in parentheses. Use simple past, present perfect simple, or present perfect continuous.

Paul,

Just a quick note to tell you how I'm doing. I ¹ __*arrived*__ (arrive) here five days ago, and I ² _____ (work) hard ever since. Lots of trees were destroyed by a fire last year, so we ³ _____ (plant) trees all week. We are working in teams, and each team has 100 trees to plant. We ⁴ _____ (not finish) yet, but we ⁵ _____ (plant) 80 already.

I ⁶ _____ (meet) Evan Leander yesterday. He's the man who organized the project, so it ⁷ _____ (be) pretty exciting to talk to him.

I'm off to work! Take care.

Janelle

Fun Spot

How many words can you make in five minutes? (Each letter must "touch" another letter in the cube.) Examples *meal, has*

A	H	R	T
S	U	A	N
I	M	E	E
T	L	A	D

A	S	T	O
C	E	R	H
I	N	A	Y
F	L	D	M

7 By design

✔ Design in public spaces and cars
✔ Passive forms: Modals; *so / such (a)...that*

1 ▷ Reading

a Look at the pictures. What do you think are the difficulties of building a suspension bridge? A dam? A tunnel?

b Read the descriptions. What are the "engineering challenges" for each structure?

ENGINEERING
CHALLENGES

BRIDGES

A suspension bridge is usually built where a long distance has to be spanned. The roadway is suspended by cables that transfer the weight of the roadway to the towers at either end.

The Akashi Kaikyo Bridge in Japan is 12,828 feet long and links the city of Kobe with Awaji-shima Island. It was built to resist winds of up to 180 miles per hour, hurricanes, and sometimes earthquakes. The bridge was originally designed to be 12,825 feet long. But on January 17, 1995, the great Hanshin Earthquake stretched the bridge an additional three feet.

DAMS

Throughout history, dams have prevented flooding, irrigated farmland, and generated tremendous amounts of electricity. They can be built in different ways, depending on the location. The most common type of dam is an embankment dam, such as the Aswan High Dam, in Egypt, which allows the water from the Nile River to be captured during rainy seasons and released during times of drought.

Embankment dams rely on their heavy weight to resist the force of the water. They have a waterproof center that prevents water from coming through. Nevertheless, all dams must be maintained as they get older. Without proper maintenance, the concrete can crack.

TUNNELS

It took engineers thousands of years to perfect the art of digging tunnels. One of the problems in tunnel construction is supporting the ground while the tunnel is being made. Because of this, the least complicated tunnels are made through rock, which does not have to be supported. Underwater tunnels are particularly hard to construct, since water must be held back while the tunnel is being made. Today, prefabricated tunnel sections can be floated into position, sunk, and attached to other sections.

c Read the descriptions again. Then answer the questions.
1 What are three parts of a suspension bridge?
2 Why did the Akashi Kaikyo Bridge become longer?
3 What are three things that dams do?
4 What are two ways that embankment dams resist water?
5 What kind of tunnels are the easiest to construct?

d What structures in your area were difficult to build? Why?

2 ▶ Focus on Grammar

a Look at the chart. Number the parts of the statements and questions in the correct order. Then underline three more examples of passive forms of modal verbs in the final paragraph on page 53.

1 Statements: __ be __ modal verb _1_ subject __ past participle
2 Questions: __ be __ modal verb __ past participle __ subject __ (question word)

Passive forms: Modals		
Dams	**can**	**be built** in different ways.
All dams	**must**	**be maintained** as they get older.
A large distance	**has to**	**be spanned** by a suspension bridge.
	Should a dam	**be built** in this area?
How	**can** the ground	**be supported**?

b Use the cues to write statements or questions in the passive.

1 a new bridge / will / build / next year — _A new bridge will be built next year_.
2 those old buildings / can / save — _____?
3 the dam / ought to / repair / soon — _____.
4 the building / had to / destroy — _____.
5 the project / should / discuss / with the neighbors — _____?
6 the new school / will / finish / in time — _____?

c What buildings should be saved, improved, or built in your community?

3 ▶ Listening

a Look at the picture. What do you think was the most difficult aspect of building the Brooklyn Bridge?

b **AUDIO** Listen to the tour guide. What is the answer to the question above?

c **AUDIO** Listen again. Fill in the missing information in the tour guide's notes.

d How do you think things would be different if the bridge were built today?

The construction of the Brooklyn Bridge, 1880s

The Brooklyn Bridge

• completed in [1]_____ cost [2]_____
• designed by John Roebling, but managed by [3]_____.
• workers got decompression sickness from working [4]_____
• Washington R became ill, directed construction from [5]_____ using a telescope. [6]_____ gave orders to workers
• bridge was important because [7]_____
• cost: [8]_____ to walk across the bridge, 10 cents for a one-horse wagon, 5 cents for a horse / cow

4 ▶ Vocabulary: Landmarks

a Work in pairs or small groups. Do you know where these landmarks are?

the Golden Gate Bridge   the Statue of Liberty   the Arc de Triomphe   the Suez Canal
Red Square   the Eiffel Tower   the Channel Tunnel   the Sky Dome
the Washington Monument   the Itaipú Dam   the Trevi Fountain

the Trevi Fountain   the Washington Monument   the Sky Dome

> ▼ **Help Desk**
>
> Use *the* with most landmarks, but not with *square*.
>
> **the** Eiffel Tower, **the** Washington Monument
>
> But: *Red Square*

b Fill in the blanks with the correct word.

arch   canal   dome   square   tower   monument   fountain   statue

1   *monument*
2   _____
3   _____
4   _____
5   _____
6   _____
7   _____
8   _____

c Think of an example of each type of structure in your area.

5 ▶ *KnowHow*: Silent consonants

a The *k* in *know* and the *g* in *design* are not pronounced—they are silent. Circle the silent consonants in these words.

right   wrong   honest   daughter   answer   half   foreign
hour   would   thumb   knee   listen   weight   Wednesday

b **AUDIO** Listen and check your answers.

c Write a sentence using as many of the words above as possible. Dictate the sentence to a partner. Can your partner spell the words correctly?

6 ▷ Language in Action: Likes and dislikes

a **AUDIO** Who likes the building? Who doesn't? Listen. Then read.

Olivia: What's that building over there?

Kim: That? Oh, that's the new art museum.

Olivia: Hmm…. It's quite an unusual building, isn't it?

Kim: Yes, it sure is. I'm afraid I don't think much of it. But then I'm not a big fan of modern architecture.

Olivia: What do you think of it, Kurt?

Kurt: Well, you know, I couldn't stand it at first, but now I don't mind it so much. It has its good points. It's not particularly attractive from the outside, but it's very nice inside.

Kim: Would you like to take a look?

Olivia: Sure. That would be interesting.

b Write four more expressions from the conversation in the chart below.

LIKE	DISLIKE	PARTLY LIKE
I really like it. I like it a lot / very much.	I don't really like it. 1 _____ 2 _____ I can't stand it. (strong)	It's OK, I guess. It's not too bad. 3 _____ 4 _____

Note: To make your opinion less direct, use *a little* or *a bit* before a negative adjective.
I don't really like that building. It's a little dark. (= It's dark.) Use *not very* or *not particularly* before a positive adjective. *It's not particularly attractive.* (= not attractive)

c Work in small groups. Look at these buildings. What do you think of them? Ask each other for opinions. Use the expressions in the chart where appropriate.

Example A: *What do you think of this building?*
          B: *I really like it. What about you?*
          A: *Hmm. It's OK, I guess. It's a little…*

d In groups, agree on two buildings in your community that you like and two that you dislike.

56

7 ▶ Writing

a Read the description. Why does the writer like Plaza Olavide?

b Choose a public place and write a description of it. Include information about…

location
physical appearance
activities that happen there
what you like or don't like about it

c Exchange papers with a partner. Ask two questions about the place your partner has chosen.

-2-

I am writing from one of my favorite places in all of Madrid — the Plaza Olavide. It's a small square, except it's not really square! It's round, with different streets around it, like a wheel. The traffic goes under the plaza, and there's a parking garage under it, too, so the plaza itself is just for pedestrians.

It's like a little oasis in the center of the city, especially in the morning when it's fairly quiet. It actually feels like being in a small village rather than in the middle of a big city. There are apartment buildings all around it, and sometimes you see people opening the windows to let in the air from the plaza. After school, children play in the small grassy area in the middle. And there are cafés and restaurants where you can enjoy

8 ▶ Speaking

a Work in small groups. Imagine you have to design a public park at the corner of two busy streets in your area. Discuss how to make your park an attractive public place. Use the list to help you decide how the park should be designed.

Access:	Entrance(s), walkways, bus stops, parking
Comfort:	Attractive features (plants, water, grass…), seating, safety
Uses and activities:	Who will use the park?, What kind of activities are there? (playground, live music, art…)

b Draw a plan of your park.

c Present your plan to the class. Explain the reasons for the decisions you made.

9 ▶ Listening

a Look at the pictures. What words would you use to describe each vehicle?

_____   _____   _____

b [AUDIO] Listen. Number the pictures in the order you hear them described.

c [AUDIO] Listen again. Which features does each person mention? Complete the chart.

color   gas mileage   reliability   size   speed   style

#1	#2	#3
beauty, color color,	gm, style. size	gm. size, style. colour, speed.

d What kinds of cars do you like or dislike? Why?

10 ▶ Vocabulary: The car

a [AUDIO] Look at the picture. Try to fill in the missing car parts. Then listen and check.

seat belt   engine   headlights   tire   passenger seat   steering wheel

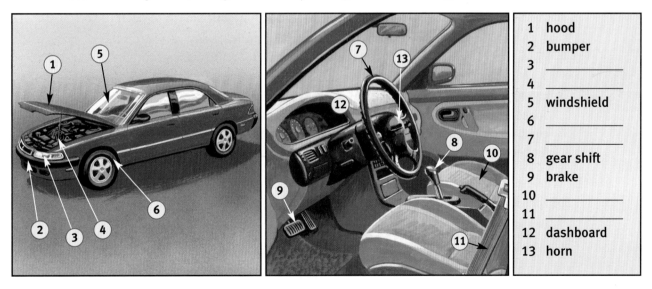

1	hood
2	bumper
3	_____
4	_____
5	windshield
6	_____
7	_____
8	gear shift
9	brake
10	_____
11	_____
12	dashboard
13	horn

b Work with a partner. Cover the words. Name as many car parts as you can.

Focus on Grammar

a Look at the chart. Then complete the rules using the words below.

that   so   such (a)

1   Use _____ before an adjective or a phrase with *much* or *many*.
2   Use _____ before a noun or a noun phrase.
3   To introduce a result clause use _____.

So / Such (a)...that		
Exclamations / emphasis	That car was	**so heavy!**
	I had	**so much stuff (so many things)!**
	That was	**such a beauty!**
	They were	**such great cars!**
With result clauses	It was **so heavy**	**that** it got terrible gas mileage.
	It was **such a great car**	**that** everybody wanted one.

Note: In exclamations, *so* and *such* are usually stressed: *That car was so heavy! It was such a heavy car!*

b Put *so* or *such* into each sentence to add emphasis.

1   The truck was ^{so} reliable.
2   My sister is a careful driver.
3   The van holds many people.
4   This is an unusual car.
5   The town has narrow streets.
6   The seats are comfortable.
7   Newer cars get good gas mileage.
8   This car was a good deal.

c Now add a *that* clause to each sentence above. Use your own ideas.

Example   *The truck was so reliable that we kept it for 20 years.*

12 Speaking

a Work in small groups. Imagine you are a car salesperson. The cars you sell have all of the features listed. Discuss which four features you would emphasize to each of the customers (1–3).

1   A sales representative who drives up to 300 miles a day
2   A parent buying a car for his or her daughter—a university student
3   A limousine driver

safety features (air bags, car alarm)   comfortable seats
space—seats five people easily   sunroof
compact size—easy to park   CD player
fuel economy—gets good gas mileage   large trunk

b Work with a partner. Role-play a conversation between the salesperson and one or more of the customers.

Begin like this:

Salesperson: May I help you?
Customer: Yes, I'm looking for a car that...

13 ▸ Listening: Song

a AUDIO Look at the picture and listen to the song without reading the lyrics. What do you think the song is about?

b Read the song and the explanations in the glossary. Discuss the questions.

1 What kind of car is the girl driving?
2 Whose car is it?
3 Does she still have the car at the end of the song? Why or why not?

c AUDIO Now listen to the song again. Discuss the questions.

1 What effect does the car have on…
   the driver?
   the other girls?
   the boys?
2 Why do you think the car has such an effect on people?
3 Do cars still have this kind of effect?

Glossary

cruisin' (cruising) = driving around slowly with no particular destination

T-Bird = A Thunderbird, a car popular in the U.S. in the 1960s

Indy 500 = The Indianapolis 500-mile race, a car race

an ace = a person who is very good at something

wild-goose chase = an attempt to get something you can't get

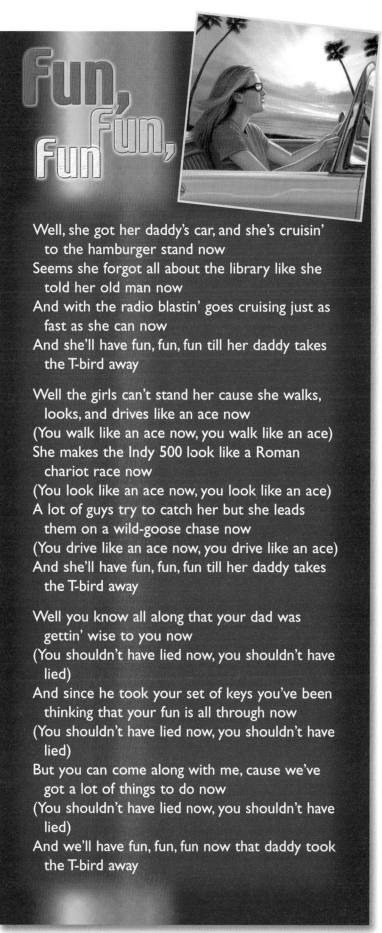

Fun, Fun, Fun

Well, she got her daddy's car, and she's cruisin'
   to the hamburger stand now
Seems she forgot all about the library like she
   told her old man now
And with the radio blastin' goes cruising just as
   fast as she can now
And she'll have fun, fun, fun till her daddy takes
   the T-bird away

Well the girls can't stand her cause she walks,
   looks, and drives like an ace now
(You walk like an ace now, you walk like an ace)
She makes the Indy 500 look like a Roman
   chariot race now
(You look like an ace now, you look like an ace)
A lot of guys try to catch her but she leads
   them on a wild-goose chase now
(You drive like an ace now, you drive like an ace)
And she'll have fun, fun, fun till her daddy takes
   the T-bird away

Well you know all along that your dad was
   gettin' wise to you now
(You shouldn't have lied now, you shouldn't have
   lied)
And since he took your set of keys you've been
   thinking that your fun is all through now
(You shouldn't have lied now, you shouldn't have
   lied)
But you can come along with me, cause we've
   got a lot of things to do now
(You shouldn't have lied now, you shouldn't have
   lied)
And we'll have fun, fun, fun now that daddy took
   the T-bird away

8 Special offer

✔ Services and advertising
✔ *Have / get* + object + past participle; verb + object + infinitive

1 ▶ Speaking

a Look at the pictures of these mobile services. Why do you think each service is successful?

Collapsible Cinemobil is popular in rural areas in France

Mobile Fitness Center in Chicago: Why go to the gym if the gym will come to you?

This converted fire truck is perfect for kids' parties and swimming lessons

b Work with a partner. Imagine a service that would be useful for one or more of these groups. Then present your ideas to the class.

traveling business executives   tourists   parents with young children   teachers

2 ▶ Listening

Veronica Ward
Personal Assistant

❀ errands
❀ shopping
❀ house sitting
❀ gift buying
❀ dog walking
❀ home organization
❀ party and event planning

Veronica Ward
Personal Assistant

(973) 555-2300

You need it.... We do it!

(973) 555-2300

a Look at the business card. Discuss the questions.
   1   What kind of services does Veronica Ward offer?
   2   Why do you think people might use her services?

b **AUDIO** Listen to the interview with Veronica. Number the topics in the order they are mentioned.
   _5_ how she finds clients
   _3_ how she helps people in their homes
   _1_ what she does in general *PO, cleaness.*
   _2_ why she started the service
   _4_ the most interesting thing she's been asked to do

c **AUDIO** Listen again. Note what Veronica says about each topic above.

d Would a service like Veronica's be useful for you? Why (not)?

▼ **Help Desk**

Errands are short trips to get / do something. (to the store, the post office...)

People *do errands* or *run errands*.

3 ▶ Focus on Grammar

a Look at the chart. Then choose the correct ending for the sentence.

To *have* or *get something done* means…
(to do something yourself / to arrange for somebody else to do something).

Have / get + object + past participle			
Why do the work myself if I can	**have**	**it**	**done** by somebody else?
We didn't want to cook, so we	**had**	**a pizza**	**delivered.**
I'm going to the cleaners to	**get**	**my pants**	**cleaned.**
My watch broke, but I haven't	**gotten**	**it**	**fixed** yet.

b Complete the sentences with *have / get* + object + past participle. Use the words in parentheses.

1 You really ought to *have your eyes checked* by a doctor. (check / your eyes)
2 I'm going to _____. (do / my nails)
3 Do you know where I can _____? (fix / the car)
4 She _____ for the wedding. (make / the dress)
5 You look different. Did you _____? (cut / your hair)
6 We have already _____ by professional painters. (paint / our apartment)

c What can you have or get done at each of these places? Use the words below.

make   clean   cut
do   send   fix
wash

d What kinds of services are popular where you live?

4 ▶ *KnowHow*: Vocabulary learning

a Read the quotations from language students about how they learn new words and expressions. Which of the strategies have you used?

1 "I like to organize words in lots of different ways. I make diagrams with lots of lines and curves and circles. It helps me remember words that are related to each other."
2 "I work with people who speak English. Whenever I hear a word or an expression that I don't know, I ask them to repeat it, and I write it down in my notebook."
3 "I read magazines and newspapers in English. When I find a word I want to know, I look it up in the dictionary and write it down."
4 "I try to use the new expressions I've learned as soon as possible. Once I've used a word or an expression a couple of times, I can remember it."

b Work with a partner. Say what you do to record and remember new words. Can you add a strategy to the list above? Share your ideas with the class.

5 ▶ Vocabulary: Damaged goods

a Match the sentences (1–6) with the pictures (A–F).

1 A button has **come off** the shirt. Now it's **missing**. —
2 The tie is **stained**. There are **stains** on the tie. —
3 The jeans are **torn**, and there's a **hole** in the knee. —
4 Someone has **scratched** the car. There are **scratches** on the hood. —
5 The cup is **chipped** and **cracked**. —
6 The faucet is **leaking**. There's a **leak** in the faucet. —

> ▼ **Help Desk**
>
> Many words in English can be used as nouns or verbs.
>
> *There's **a leak** in the faucet.* (noun)
>
> *The faucet **is leaking**.* (verb)

b Work with a partner. Say what you would do about each problem above.

Example *If a button came off my shirt, I would sew it back on.*

6 ▶ Language in Action: Irritation

a AUDIO Listen. Why is Rob angry? What mistake has he made?

b AUDIO Listen again. Check the expressions that you hear in the chart.

c Work with a partner. Imagine that you are having a problem with something you just bought or had repaired. Role-play a conversation, using the prompts below.

Example A: *I can't believe it. / Oh, no!*
B: *What's the problem?*
A: *(Explain your problem.) It makes me mad / drives me crazy*
B: *That's terrible. You should…*
A: *I will, but I don't know why they don't…*

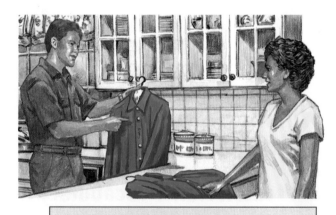

EXPRESSING IRRITATION
__ It's ridiculous!
__ It (really) makes me mad.
__ That's the last time I…
__ I won't…again.
__ It (really) drives me crazy.
__ I'm fed up with it.
__ I don't know why they don't…
__ Why don't they…
__ I can't believe it!

Note: Be careful! These expressions are not usually used with the person you're irritated with. They are often used when you are complaining to a different person.

7 ▶ Writing

a Read the letter. Who is it to and who is it from? What is the problem?

> 34 Babcock Way
> Landsdale, GA 98765
>
> Customer Service Department
> DF Sports, Inc.
> 2370 Franklin Avenue
> Everett, MN 12345
>
> June 16, 2005
>
> To Whom It May Concern:
>
> I ordered a green baseball shirt, extra large, from your company by telephone on June 6 (Reference number CX45783). Unfortunately, you have sent me a small blue shirt. I am returning it today by mail.
>
> Please send me the color and size that I ordered. If this is not available, I would appreciate it if you could credit my account for the full amount.
>
> Thank you for your attention.
>
> Sincerely,
>
> *Michael Ramos*
>
> Michael Ramos

b Look at the letter again. Answer the questions.

1 In a formal letter, where do you put…
   your address?   the name and address of the person you're writing to?   the date?
2 How does Michael begin this letter? Why?
3 How does he end the letter?

c Read the three situations (A–C). Then look at the list of expressions (1–7). Check which situation each expression might be used in.

A You are writing to a company to ask for a catalogue of their products.
B You want to get your money back for a canceled flight.
C You ordered a book on the Internet, but it hasn't arrived yet. You want to find out why it is late.

	A	B	C
1 Could you please send me…			
2 I am enclosing…			
3 I would appreciate it if you could let me know…			
4 Please credit my account.			
5 Thank you for your attention.			
6 I look forward to hearing from you.			
7 I look forward to receiving the information.			

d Choose a situation and write a letter. Use the letter above as a model for layout.

8 ▶ In Conversation

AUDIO What does Sonia think about Marilyn's decision? Listen. Then read.

Marilyn: Look at these sunglasses. Buy one pair, get one free! That's a good deal.

Sonia: That's just to get you to buy them. You don't need sunglasses. Look at the weather!

Marilyn: I know, but they're so cheap. Look at these. I think they make me look sophisticated. What do you think? Come on…I'd like you to give me some advice.

Sonia: Well, I don't think you should buy them. They don't look very good. And it says, "No refunds, no exchanges." They won't let you bring them back if you don't like them.

Salesperson: May I help you?

Marilyn: Yes. I'll take these two pairs of sunglasses.

Salesperson: OK. I'll have someone take care of that for you.

Sonia: Honestly, Marilyn!

9 ▶ Focus on Grammar

a Look at the chart. Then look at the conversation above. Find one more example of…

1 verb + object + infinitive with *to*.   2 verb + object + infinitive without *to*.

Verb + object + infinitive	
with to	
I'**d like you to give** me some advice. They **expect you to buy** things.	*advise, allow, ask, encourage, expect, forbid, force, get, give, help, invite, need, order, persuade, remind, tell, want, warn, would like, would prefer*
without to (base form)	
They won't **let you bring** them back. They **make me look** sophisticated.	*make, let, have, help*
Note: *Help* can take both forms. *I'll **help you to choose**.* OR *I'll **help you choose**.*	

b Complete the paragraph with the correct form of the verb in parentheses.

Companies that want you ¹ _to buy_ (buy) their products know what makes people ² _buy_ (buy) something. They know that attractive packaging can persuade customers ³ _____ (spend) more money, and that clever placement of the goods will get you ⁴ _____ (notice) something. A relaxed atmosphere also encourages shoppers ⁵ _____ (stay) longer in a store and lets them ⁶ _____ (examine) the goods without pressure. Most customers want salespeople ⁷ _____ (give) them information, but people don't like being forced ⁸ _____ (buy) things.

c Write realistic sentences with the endings below. Use verbs from the chart above.

study   eat fast food   pay for dinner   make friends   spend too much money

Examples *My teachers encouraged me to study. / Please let me pay for dinner!*

10 ▶ Listening

a Do you listen to radio commercials? What services and products are usually advertised?

b **AUDIO** Listen to the commercials. Circle the three products or services that are advertised.

a card store	a mattress store	a pharmacy
a restaurant	a supermarket	an online shopping service

c **AUDIO** Listen again and answer the questions.

1 Where is Mattress Matters?   _Princeton_
2 How long is the sale at Mattress Matters?   _____
3 When is the pharmacy at Superprice open? (days and time)   _____
4 What food items are mentioned in the Superprice commercial? _____
5 What does the man give his girlfriend at the beginning?   _____
   At the end?   _____
6 How do you get free delivery from whattogive.klıw?   _____

d Which commercial do you think is most effective? Why?

11 ▶ Vocabulary: Adverbs

a Look at the advertisements. Answer the questions.

1 What is each advertisement for?
2 Find adverbs in the advertisements that are similar in meaning to…
   only. _____   very. _____   nearly. _____
3 What is the difference in meaning between these two sentences?
   We only sell flowers.   *We even sell flowers.*

b Choose the correct adverb to complete each sentence.

1 This jacket was (completely / (very)) expensive, but I got it for (even / just) 49 dollars in the sale.
2 (Almost / completely) anybody can operate this sound system. (Even / Just) my six-year-old understands it.
3 The sale is (almost / very) over. Get a new car at an (incredibly / almost) good price.
4 These shoes are (completely / almost) waterproof and warm, (even / just) in snow.
5 Our suits look great on everyone. And they're at prices so low, we're (almost / incredibly) giving them away!

12 ▶ Reading

a Work with a partner. Discuss the questions.

1   How many different kinds of advertising do you encounter every day?

2   What kinds of advertising are shown in the pictures on this page?

b Read the articles quickly to find out...

1   how each form of advertising works.

2   what people think of each of them.

A

MOTION ADS MAY MAKE COMMUTE SEEM FASTER

The view outside your train window is about to get a bit more interesting. Riders on the PATH between New York and New Jersey are the first to see a new type of ad—motion picture ads.

"Certainly as they're riding through the tunnels and the tunnels are dark, normally they don't see anything," says Victoria Cross Kelly, Deputy Director of PATH. "This gives people something to look at...It's like watching a little movie while you're on the train."

The technique works kind of like those picture books you might have had as a kid. You flip the pages really fast, and it looks like a motion picture. It's like that, only in reverse, because you're the one moving while the pictures, posted on the tunnel walls, stay still. It takes between 150 and 250 pictures to make one 15-to-20 second display.

So which do passengers prefer: this new type of fast-paced advertising, or the conventional kind of advertising inside the train? "[The motion ads] are much better," says one commuter. But he admitted, "I'm not sure what they're advertising."

B

SANDWICH BOARDS IN DANGER

There's a chill in the air, and it looks like rain. The wind is blowing across Liberty Square, but Ed McCrory has seen worse. Bad weather is part of the job description for the 52-year-old sandwich board carrier. He spends most days standing on the corner of a busy street, wearing a plastic sign and handing out fliers for a clothing store.

He points to a nearby awning. "When it rains, I get under there," he confides. Thick woolen socks and thermal underwear help him stay cozy in the winter.

Sandwich boards, both manned and unmanned, are one of the oldest forms of advertising. Store owners believe they help to attract customers, especially to businesses on side streets. "We wouldn't get so much business without them," says Randy Simowitz, a clerk at the clothing store. "Customers see the sign, or get a flier, and they come on in." However, complaints from upscale businesses in the area—who view sandwich boards as bad taste—and pedestrians—who view them as a nuisance—are on the rise. City officials are discussing a proposal that would force businesses to apply for a permit and pay a fee.

McCrory isn't worried about his job. "They need me," he says confidently. "Without me, they wouldn't be in business."

c Read the articles again. Write T (true), F (false), or NI (no information).

A (motion ads):

1 These ads have been around for a long time. —
2 The ads are posted on the tunnel walls. —
3 It takes 15 to 20 pictures to make one display. —
4 40,000 people see the motion ads every day. —

B (sandwich boards):

5 Sandwich boards are only used in good weather. —
6 Ed McCrory has been working as a sandwich board carrier for 20 years. __
7 Sandwich boards have been around for a long time. —
8 Some people don't like sandwich boards. —

d Match the words with the definitions.

1 flip (A)   _1d_   a a temporary roof over an outside window or door
2 display (A)   __   b high class, expensive
3 conventional (A)   __   c an arrangement of things for people to see
4 fliers (B)   __   d turn with a quick movement
5 awning (B)   __   e traditional, usual
6 cozy (B)   __   f warm and comfortable
7 upscale (B)   __   g ads on sheets of paper

e What are some other unusual types of advertising?

13 ▶ Speaking and Writing

a Work in small groups. Choose one of the following to advertise. Decide the main points that your ad will focus on.

   an item of technology
      (an electronic dictionary, a cell phone...)
   a household item
      (a cleaning product, a kitchen utensil...)
   a service
      (a window cleaner, a car service...)
   a store
      (a clothing store, a computer store...)

b Write a one-minute radio commercial for your product or service.

c "Perform" your commercials for the class. Which commercials are most effective?

Make your windows shine with Gerry's Window Cleaning Service. We offer...

9 Mysteries and science

✔ Unsolved mysteries and scientific explanations
✔ Modals: Possibility; noun clauses

1 ▶ Reading

a Look at the pictures and the information from a guidebook. What kind of mysteries do you think these are?

b Read the article. Which mystery do you think is the most unusual?

Mysteries of the Southwest

Strange lights, dancing rocks, and abandoned settlements—the Southwestern United States has it all.

MARFA LIGHTS

Thousands of visitors come to the West Texas desert every year to witness an age-old phenomenon: tiny lights suspended in the air. It is impossible to say what they are or to see exactly where they come from.

The Ghost Lights of Marfa were first reported more than a century ago. They look a little like car headlights moving on nearby roads. But the lights have been around longer than electric lights or cars. The Apache people believed the strange lights were stars dropping to earth. Some romantics describe the lights as the torches of long-dead lovers wandering in search of one another.

DANCING ROCKS

The sight is amazing. Dozens of rocks, some weighing hundreds of pounds, seem to move by themselves on the flat mud of an ancient lakebed in Death Valley. Their tracks may be long or short, straight or curved. The mystery is, how do the rocks move? No one has ever seen a rock in motion on the flat surface, but since 1948, scientists have been trying to explain the phenomenon.

One of the first suggestions was that the wind pushes the stones. Water may be a key factor: rain makes the surface slippery and the wind pushes the rocks along. Ice occasionally forms during the winter, so the rocks may glide in sheets of ice floating in shallow water. But none of these explanations is entirely satisfactory. The research continues.

THE MYSTERY OF THE ANASAZI

The Anasazi were a numerous and sophisticated people who established a flourishing culture in the Mesa Verde area about 1,500 years ago. But in the late 1200s, the Anasazi suddenly left their homes and mysteriously moved away, taking only what they could carry on their backs.

The Anasazi must have had a good reason to leave the area, but no one really understands why they left. There have been many theories. One explanation is that a drought might have forced them to move to a different area. But this couldn't have been the only reason. They may have lost a battle with a neighboring tribe, or they could have contracted some kind of disease. Most likely, it was a combination of factors that caused the Anasazi to leave the elaborate stone cities that they built in the canyon walls.

c Which questions refer to which mystery? Write 1, 2, or 3 next to each question. Which questions are answered or discussed in section 1?

1 = Marfa Lights   2 = Dancing Rocks   3 = Anasazi

1 How do they move?   —
2 What are they?   —
3 Where did they go?   —
4 Where do they come from?   —
5 Why did they leave?   —

d Find these words in the article. Then write each word next to the correct definition.

torches   tracks   slippery   shallow   flourishing   canyon

1 growing in a successful way   *flourishing*_____
2 burning sticks that give light   _____
3 a deep valley with steep sides   _____
4 smooth and wet, easy to slide on   _____
5 not deep   _____
6 lines or marks left behind by something _____

e Work with a partner. Discuss the questions.

1 Which of the theories do you agree with? Can you think of any other explanations?
2 What other phenomena like these have you heard of?

2 ▶ Vocabulary: Expressions with *leave, move, stay,* and *take*

a Look at the diagrams. Fill in the verb that goes with each set of expressions.

**leave   move
stay   take**

①
___
at / in a place
with people
in bed, at home
awake

③
___
a place
something behind
a message for someone
the door open

②
___
to a different place
away (from home)
in / out
quickly

④
___
someone to a place
something to a place
a train / bus / flight
time to do something

b Fill in the blanks with the appropriate form of one of the verbs in 2a.

1 The Anasazi *left* their homes and _____ to a different place. They _____ very little with them.

2 I _____ my sister to the airport last week. She was _____ a flight to Europe to _____ with relatives. When we got to the airport, she realized that she had _____ her passport at home.

3 It _____ two hours to get to the remote island by boat. When the weather is bad, the boat can't _____. Nobody lives on the island anymore. The last inhabitants _____ to the mainland in the 1960s because it was too hard for them to _____ there.

3 ▶ Focus on Grammar

a Look at the chart and answer the questions.

1 You're almost sure something is true or not true. Which forms are used to express this?
2 What form of the verb follows *may / might / could / must have*?

Modals: Possibility (speculation)

Why did the Anasazi leave?

Possible	They	**may / might / could**	**have lost** a battle.
	They	**may not / might not**	**have had** enough water.
Certain / probable	They	**must**	**have had** more than one reason.
Impossible / not probable	There	**couldn't**	**have been** just one reason.

Note: To ask if something was possible, use *could have*.
Could the Anasazi have moved to better land? — Yes, they could have.

---

b Rewrite the conversations, replacing the underlined phrases with *must have*, *may have*, *might (not) have*, or *could(n't) have*. (More than one answer is sometimes possible.)

A: Did you see that strange light?
B: Yes. <u>I'm sure it was</u> an animal.
  ¹ *It must have been an animal.*

A: <u>I'm sure it wasn't</u> an animal. It was too high.
  2 _____

B: <u>Maybe it was</u> someone with a flashlight.
  3 _____

A: I guess so.

C: Where's Tony?
D: <u>Perhaps he went</u> to the gym.
  4 _____

C: <u>It's not possible that he did that.</u> The gym's closed.
  5 _____

D: Oh. Well, his bike's not here. <u>I'm sure he went</u> for a bike ride.
  6 _____

c **AUDIO** Listen to the first conversation. What do you notice about the pronunciation of *have*?

4 ▶ Listening

a Look at the picture. What do you think this story will be about?

b **AUDIO** Listen to the first part of Julie's story. Answer the questions.

1 Where did this happen?
2 What did she see?
3 What do you think it might have been?

c **AUDIO** Listen to the rest of the story. What did Julie actually see?

d **AUDIO** Listen to the first part of the story again. Who or what was…

1 depressing?
2 big and dark?
3 enormous and huge?
4 large and heavy?
5 big and ugly
6 terrified?

e Work with a partner. Retell the story, using your own words.

5 ▷ Vocabulary: Strong adjectives

a Match an adjective on the left with a stronger adjective on the right.

1	big	_1d_	a	exhausted
2	small	___	b	freezing
3	cold	___	c	furious
4	bad	___	d	huge / enormous
5	angry	___	e	amazed
6	afraid	___	f	awful / terrible
7	tired	___	g	terrified
8	surprised	___	h	tiny

b Work with a partner. Imagine you are telling a story. Invent short conversations, as in the example. Begin each conversation with one of the sentences below.

> Example   A: *My flight took 12 hours!*
> B: *You must have been tired.*
> A: *Tired? I was absolutely exhausted!*

1 I didn't sleep at all last night.
2 It was snowing, and I didn't have a jacket.
3 Yesterday, someone was following me home.
4 My daughter took the car without my permission.
5 The hotel we stayed at had 5,000 bedrooms.

> ▼ **Help Desk**
>
> *Very* isn't usually used with strong adjectives. Use *really* or *absolutely*.
>
> *I was absolutely terrified.*
> (Not: ~~I was very terrified.~~)

6 ▷ Speaking and Writing

a Think of something frightening, surprising, or unusual that happened to you (or to someone else you know). Use the questions to help you plan your story. Make notes.

1 What happened?	4 What did you do?
2 When and where did this happen?	5 How did you feel?
3 What were you doing at the time?	6 What explanation can you give?

b Work with a partner. A, tell your story. B, ask questions and take notes.

c Use your notes to write your partner's story. Write as if it had happened to you. Try to write at least one page.

d Read your partner's version of your story. Are the details correct?

e Make any necessary changes. Then work in small groups. Read the stories. Can you guess who originally told each one?

7 ▶ Reading

a Look at the pictures and the headline. Discuss the questions.

    1 What is a fossil?   2 What do paleontologists do?

b Read the article. Number the topics in order.

  __ conditions at the site   __ how the scientists work   __ recent discoveries

  __ places Sereno has been   __ Sereno's life and work

UNRAVELING THE MYSTERIES OF
FOSSILS

Paul Sereno is a professor of paleontology (the study of fossils) at the University of Chicago. He has made it his life's work to search for unknown dinosaurs. He has led dozens of expeditions to remote areas of the world to discover what creatures lived on the earth hundreds of millions of years ago.

Q: Where have you been to look for dinosaur remains?

A: We've been to Niger, Morocco, India, Mongolia… Some places are so remote that the land has hardly been disturbed at all. We've found out that desert conditions are often excellent for fossil formation.

Q: What do you do when you find bones or fossils?

A: We don't excavate immediately. If you just dig up the bones and go home, you leave half of the story in the ground. First, we make maps of the site. Then we study the rock that the bones are preserved in, draw pictures of the bones, and collect other fossils we find nearby. We try to figure out how the animal died, whether it was alone or with a group, what other plants and animals lived at the same time, and things like that.

Q: Are you discovering completely new dinosaurs?

A: Yes! We're finding new species all the time. In Africa, we found the remains of several large ones, including a 70-foot long plant eater we called Jobaria. We also found the world's largest crocodile: forty feet long, with jaws as long as my body!

Q: What are the working conditions like?

A: Pretty intense! For example, in the Sahara, we were digging bones out of rock in the desert with the sun and the sand, and daily temperatures of 125 degrees. It's an experience of a lifetime, but you have to be passionate about dinosaurs to do this.

c Read the article again. List examples in the article of the following items.

    1 four places Paul Sereno's team has been on expeditions   _____

    2 four things they do before excavating   _____

    3 three things scientists try to find out at the site   _____

    4 two types of remains they found in Africa   _____

    5 three conditions they deal with on expeditions   _____

d Make a list of words in the article that are related to dinosaurs and paleontology.

e Would you like to do this kind of work? Why or why not?

8 ▷ Focus on Grammar

a Look at the noun clauses in the chart, and complete the rules.

1 Noun clauses can begin with ___*question words*___, _____, or
_____.

2 Noun clauses are used after verbs like _____*figure out*_____, _____,
_____, and _____.

Noun clauses

	Main clause	Noun clause
Question words	The scientists try to figure out	**how** the animal died.
	They don't know	**what** other animals lived at the same time.
whether / if	They want to find out	**whether** it was alone or in a group.
that	Sereno thinks	**that** desert conditions are good for fossil formation.

Note: *That* is often left out of a noun clause, especially in conversation: *He says (that) it's true.*

b Fill in the blanks with a question word, *whether / if*, or *that*. More than one answer is sometimes possible.

1 We know ___*that*___ dinosaurs existed years ago, but they suddenly disappeared. Nobody knows exactly _____ this happened. Some scientists believe _____ they died when a meteor hit the earth.

2 I wonder _____ you could help me. I'm not sure _____ floor I'm supposed to go to.

3 I'm sorry, but I can't understand _____ you're saying.

4 I know _____ the parade starts at the park, but I can't remember _____ it's at ten o'clock or eleven o'clock.

▼ **Help Desk**

Remember to use statement word order (not question word order) after question words and *if / whether* in noun clauses.

I don't know what they're studying. (Not: ~~I don't know what are they studying.~~)

c Complete the sentences with a noun clause. Then compare your answers with a partner.

1 For centuries, people have looked up at the stars and wondered _____.

2 I've always wanted to know
_____.

3 People always ask me _____.

4 Before I studied English, I didn't realize
_____.

5 I can't decide _____.

"I know what I am, but I can't pronounce it."

74

9 ▶ Speaking

a Work in small groups. Discuss the quiz. Try to agree on an answer for each question.

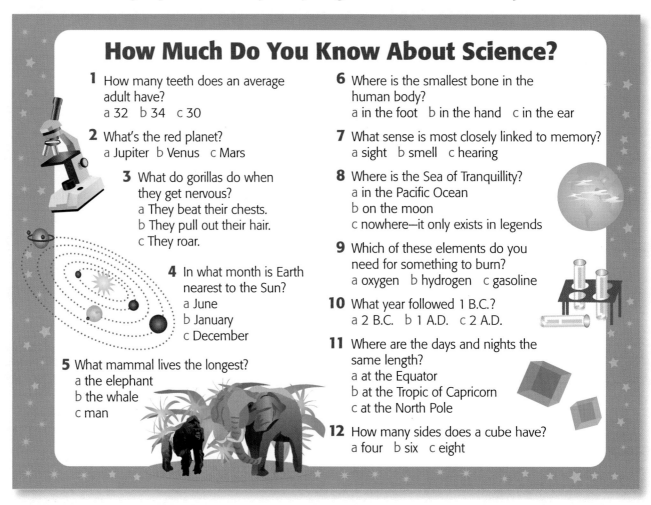

How Much Do You Know About Science?

1 How many teeth does an average adult have?
a 32 b 34 c 30

2 What's the red planet?
a Jupiter b Venus c Mars

3 What do gorillas do when they get nervous?
a They beat their chests.
b They pull out their hair.
c They roar.

4 In what month is Earth nearest to the Sun?
a June
b January
c December

5 What mammal lives the longest?
a the elephant
b the whale
c man

6 Where is the smallest bone in the human body?
a in the foot b in the hand c in the ear

7 What sense is most closely linked to memory?
a sight b smell c hearing

8 Where is the Sea of Tranquillity?
a in the Pacific Ocean
b on the moon
c nowhere—it only exists in legends

9 Which of these elements do you need for something to burn?
a oxygen b hydrogen c gasoline

10 What year followed 1 B.C.?
a 2 B.C. b 1 A.D. c 2 A.D.

11 Where are the days and nights the same length?
a at the Equator
b at the Tropic of Capricorn
c at the North Pole

12 How many sides does a cube have?
a four b six c eight

b Check your answers on page 119. Who knows the most about science?

10 ▶ *KnowHow*: Vowel sounds and spelling

a **AUDIO** Listen to the words. Underline the vowel sounds in each word. What do you notice about sounds and spelling in English?

/ eɪ /	place, rain, break
/ i /	free, theme, mean
/ aɪ /	science, drive, buy
/ u /	food, Sue, prove

b **AUDIO** Try to put these words in the chart above. Then listen and check your answers.

brake cool fly great group key guy leave mail meat
scene size stay steel weight suit wild zoo high move

c Look back at the quiz in section 9. Find two more words to add to each row in the chart above.

11 ▶ Listening

a Discuss the questions.

1 Is it possible to travel at the speed of light?

2 Why do people yawn when they see someone yawning?

b [AUDIO] Listen to the radio program. What answers do the scientists give for the questions above?

c [AUDIO] Listen again. Do the statements in the chart agree with the theories presented in the program? Check *yes* or *no*.

	Yes	No
1 Some day, we will be able to travel at the speed of light.		N
2 In a spaceship traveling at the speed of light, time would go more slowly.	Y	
3 Scientists are sure they know why people yawn.		N
4 Yawning is contagious.	Y	
5 In prehistoric times, yawning was probably a social behavior.		Y

d Work with a partner. What did you learn from the radio program that you did not know before? Think of a question that you would like to ask the people on the program.

12 ▶ Language in Action: Explanations

a [AUDIO] Listen again to part of the radio program. Check the expressions that you hear.

ASKING IF SOMEONE UNDERSTANDS

___ Do you understand?

___ (Do you) see what I mean?

SAYING YOU DON'T UNDERSTAND	**SAYING YOU UNDERSTAND**
___ Sorry, but I don't understand.	___ I see.
___ I don't get it. (*informal*)	___ I get it. (*informal*)
___ What do you mean?	___ That makes sense.
___ What I don't understand is….	___ Now I see what you mean.
___ I still don't understand….	

b Work with a partner. **A**, try to explain one of the following (or something else that you understand.) Check that your partner understands. **B**, ask for more explanations if necessary.

Why the moon seems to get bigger and smaller every month   **How a car or a bicycle works**

How a chain letter works   **How money earns interest**

Units 7–9 Review

Grammar

1 ▶ Read the article. What do some scientists believe the pyramid might be? Why?

UNDERWATER JAPANESE RUINS

There is an underwater pyramid located off the coast of the island of Yonaguni, Japan that remains a mystery. It was discovered in 1985. Some scientists believe that it is a natural rock formation that may have been changed by the people of an ancient civilization. Other scientists say that it must have been made by man. As evidence of this, they note that tools were found near the pyramid.

Tests show that the formation may be 10,000 years old and that it has been under water for 6,000 years. If this structure was made by man, it indicates the existence of an ancient civilization much older, for example, than that of the Egyptians.

---

2 ▶ Rewrite the sentences in the passive.

1 They have to study the construction of the pyramid more.
The construction of the pyramid has to be studied more.

2 No one can solve the mystery of the pyramid.

_____

3 Someone should take more photographs underwater.

_____

4 They must find more experts to study the pyramid.

_____

5 They should study the ruins more thoroughly.

_____

3 ▶ Combine these sentences, using *so* or *such* and a result clause.

1 The shoes were really cheap. I had to buy them. *The shoes were so cheap that I had to buy them.*

2 That advertising campaign was effective. The company kept using it.

_____

3 We waited in line for a long time. We were exhausted.

_____

4 They were unusual photographs. Everybody noticed them.

_____

4 ▶ Complete the sentences with a form of the expression *have something done*. Use the cues in parentheses.

1 Ted and Vera Wilson have *had a lot of work done* (a lot of work / do) on their old house recently.

2 Ted _____ (roof / repair) last month.

3 At the moment they _____ (house / paint).

4 They _____ (new kitchen / not finish) yet.

5 When everything is finished, Vera _____ (photographs / take) for the *Fix Up Your Home* magazine.

5 ▶ Complete the e-mail with *to* or *N*. (N=nothing)

Favor		

From: petet@net.khw
To: harryrj@net.khw
Subject: favor

Hi, Harry. I need a favor. I didn't get an invitation to the opening of the Andel Tower. I think they forgot ¹_____ send it to me. I don't want ²_____ call them myself, so I'd like you ³_____ ask Tami if they'll let me ⁴_____ come without an invitation. Please have her ⁵_____ send me an e-mail if it's OK.
Thanks,
Pete

6 ▶ Rewrite these sentences. Use *must have, might have,* or *could have.*

A: I'm sure they forgot to send Pete an invitation to the opening.
They must have forgotten to send
Pete an invitation.

B: I'm sure they didn't forget. He's the architect.

_____

A: Maybe they didn't have Pete's address.

_____

B: Or maybe the invitation got lost in the mail.

_____

A: Anyway, I'm sure Pete was pretty mad!

_____

7 ▶ Combine the sentences using a noun clause.

1 Is advertising effective? —I'm not sure.
I'm not sure whether/if advertising is
effective.

2 Why did he leave? —I don't know.

_____.

3 How can we solve this problem? —Let's talk about it.

_____.

4 Is the Science Museum on Grant Street? —I don't remember.

_____.

5 What time is the party? —I will ask Vinny.

_____.

Vocabulary

8 ▶ Complete the letter with the words below. There are two words you don't need to use.

hood   brakes   tear   cracks
tower   leak   take   seat belts

I am writing to complain about the vacation with your company. The hotel was very beautiful. Our room was high up in an old ¹ *tower* with good views, but there were many problems. First, we had to ² _____ our luggage up four flights of stairs by ourselves. There were big ³ _____ in the windows of our room, and there was a ⁴ _____ in the bathroom sink. There was something wrong with the

⁵ _____ of the car you provided, which made it very hard to stop. The car was unsafe because there weren't any ⁶ _____ in the car.   Yours, Ned Johnstone

9 ▶ Replace the underlined phrases with suitable strong adjectives. More than one answer is possible.

1 Their new SUV is ~~really big~~.   *enormous*

2 She was <u>very angry</u> when she saw the mess!

3 The house was <u>really cold</u> because we had no electricity.

4 They were <u>extremely tired</u> after the long hike.

5 Weren't you <u>very surprised</u> to see Thomas back in town?

6 Our apartment is <u>extremely small</u>, but it's comfortable.

7 It was a horrible experience. I was <u>very afraid</u>.

Recycling Center

10 ▶ Report what the people said. Use the cues.

1 "Please help me," he said to me. He wanted *me to help him.*

2 "Take a lot of pictures," they said to her. They told _____.

3 "Leave the room at once!" we said to them. We told _____.

4 "Could you lend me that book?" she said to me. She asked _____.

5 "Please tell me your plans," she said to us. She asked _____.

Fun Spot

Use the clues to fill in the words. (The letter *a* has been filled in.) When you have found all of the words, make a sentence.

a __ = one

__ a __ = isn't now

__ __ a __ = not this

a __ a __ __ __ __ = remarkable, wonderful

__ a __ __ __ a __ __ = large structure that people notice

10 Mind your manners

✔ Misunderstandings and manners
✔ Reported speech; *would have, should have*

1 Listening

a Work with a partner. Discuss the questions.

1 Do you watch soap operas on TV? Do you like them?
2 Look at the pictures. What do you think is happening in this soap opera?

b **AUDIO** Listen to the conversations. Answer the question below each picture.

2 Who do you think these people are?

1 Why is Amanda worried?

c **AUDIO** Listen again. Answer the questions.

1 What strange things has Daniel been saying and doing?
2 What advice does Tiffany give Amanda?
3 Why did Daniel plan the surprise?
4 What is Amanda worried about, and what does Daniel say?

3 Where are Daniel and Amanda going?

d Why do you think soap operas are popular?

2 ▶ Focus on Grammar

a Look at the chart. Compare the words people said (direct speech) with how they were reported (reported speech). Find examples of…

1 changes in tense.   2 changes in pronouns.   3 changes in word order.

Reported speech		
Direct speech		*Reported speech*
"It's a secret."	He said (that)	it **was** a secret.
"My wife doesn't know."		his wife **didn't** know.
"I can't tell you about it."		he **couldn't** tell me about it.
"I'm going downtown."		he **was going** downtown.
"We'll miss the plane."		they **would** miss the plane.
"I haven't been there."		he **hadn't been** there.
"I wanted it to be a surprise."		he **had wanted** it to be a surprise.
Questions		
"Where is Daniel?"	She asked (me, him…)	where Daniel **was.**
"Did you see him?"		whether they **had seen** him.
"Is everything OK?"		if everything **was** OK.

b Rewrite the following sentences in reported speech.

1 "I'm staying home." She said *she was staying home*_____.
2 "It'll cost about a thousand dollars." The man told me _____.
3 "We haven't finished." They said _____.
4 "What time is the party?" Fred asked me _____.
5 "Do they want any money?" I wanted to know _____.
6 "We don't have it in your size." The saleswoman told me_____.
7 "Have you done this kind of work before?" The interviewer asked Lynn

   _____.
8 "I can't do anything about it." He said _____.
9 "Lynn went to work." Pam said _____.
10 "Why did you leave the job?" They asked me _____.

c **AUDIO** Listen to the conversations. Then describe each conversation in reported speech.

Example   *The man asked the woman if she had ever been to the United States before.*

d Write the dialogue that took place for the reported conversation.

Ms. Cosby asked Stephen if he had done this kind of work before. Stephen said he hadn't, but he was willing to learn. Ms. Cosby said she was sure he would learn quickly, and asked him when he could start. He said he couldn't start until Monday.

Ms. Cosby: *Have you done this kind of work before?*_____
Stephen: _____
Ms. Cosby: _____
Stephen: _____

e Work with a partner. Describe a conversation that you had in the past. Use reported speech. Here are some ideas:

a job interview   a first meeting   a misunderstanding   a surprising telephone call

3 ▶ Vocabulary: Speaking verbs

a Look at the chart. Then complete the poem with *say, explain, tell,* or *talk*.

Say / explain something to somebody:	*Please explain the situation to me again.*
Talk to somebody:	*I was talking to a friend the other day.*
Tell / ask somebody something:	*Can I ask you a question?*
Tell (somebody) a lie, the truth, a story, a secret:	*Please tell me the truth. Don't tell lies.*

I don't know what I've done
Please ¹_____ hello to me
You won't ²_____ me what's wrong
Why won't you ³_____ to me

I'll ⁴_____ you how I feel
I want to ⁵_____ you why
I can ⁶_____ it all
I won't ⁷_____ you a lie

b **AUDIO** Listen and check your answers.

4 ▶ Speaking and Writing

a Work with a partner. Discuss what is happening in each of these scenes from soap operas. Answer the questions. Invent names and use your imagination!

  Who are the people?   Where are they?   How do they feel? Why?
  What are they saying? What is going to happen next?

b Choose one of the scenes. Work with a partner. Write a conversation for the scene. It should last at least one minute.

A

B

C

c Work in small groups. Act out your scenes.

5 ▶ Language in Action: Misunderstandings

a **AUDIO** Look at the picture and listen to the conversation. What is the misunderstanding? Why did it happen?

b **AUDIO** Listen again. Check the expressions that you hear.

CLARIFYING	UNDERSTANDING
___ I don't think (that) you understood what I meant.	___ Oh, you mean…?
___ That's not what I said. I'm sorry!	___ I thought you said / meant….
___ I didn't mean / say….	
___ I meant / said….	
___ What I was trying to say was….	

c Work with a partner. Write endings for the conversations below. Then practice them.

1 A: Let's wait here for now.
    B: An hour! I can't wait that long.

2 C: My grandfather sells rugs.
    D: Rocks? For gardens?

6 ▶ *KnowHow*: Learning styles and preferences

a Read the statements and decide how much each statement applies to you. Check the appropriate boxes. Then add up your score and find out what kind of learner you are.

b Work in small groups. Using the explanations for your scores, think of one or two things you could do to improve your learning.

What kind of learner are you?

	No, not at all true	Not really true	Somewhat true	Yes, very true
1 I enjoy speaking in pairs and groups in class.	4	3	2	1
2 I get frustrated when I don't understand everything I hear.	1	2	3	4
3 I don't like to speak English because I feel self-conscious about my mistakes.	1	2	3	4
4 I like to try out new words, even if I get them wrong.	4	3	2	1
5 I often ask to be corrected.	1	2	3	4
6 I like to know the meaning of every word that I read.	1	2	3	4
7 I don't worry about making mistakes.	4	3	2	1
8 When I listen to English, I can usually figure out the general idea.	4	3	2	1

YOUR SCORE [ ]

8–16   You are a risk taker. You might need to pay more attention to accuracy if you want to improve.

16–23 You take some risks, but you also pay attention to accuracy.

24–32 You don't like to take risks. You might need to worry less about mistakes to help you learn more English.

Listening

a   Think of some examples of good manners. Do you think good manners are going out of style?

b   AUDIO Listen to some people discussing manners that are going out of style. What types of behavior do they discuss?

c   AUDIO Listen again. What are the people talking about in each case?

	Opening car doors	Holding doors open	Thank-you notes	First names
1 I love it. I feel really special.	✓			
2 Well, you wouldn't anyway!				
3 I think that's basic good manners.				
4 People don't even expect it any more.				
5 "What a nice thing to do!"				
6 I always felt really strange doing that.				
7 There's no real rule.				

Speaking

a   Work in small groups. Discuss how you would rate the items 1–8 and fill in the chart. Then add your own ideas for items 9–12.

   1 = definitely good manners
   2 = good manners, but not essential
   3 = common bad manners
   4 = definitely bad manners

	1	2	3	4
1 Opening car doors for people				
2 Writing thank-you notes				
3 Eating or drinking on the street				
4 Honking the car horn at others				
5 Chewing gum in public				
6 Double-parking				
7 Asking for permission to smoke				
8 Taking food without asking in someone's house				
9	✓			
10		✓		
11			✓	
12				✓

b   Compare your answers with other groups. Which types of behaviors do you agree on?

Focus on Grammar

a Look at these sentences from the conversation in section 7. Choose the correct answers.

She should have apologized. That's what I would have done.

1   The woman (apologized / didn't apologize).
2   The speaker thinks the woman's behavior was (right / wrong).

b Look at the chart. What form of the verb follows *should have* and *would have*?

Would have, should have		
Statements	She **should have held** the door open. She **shouldn't have been** so rude.	I **would have apologized.** I **wouldn't have done** that.

Questions	What **should** she **have done**?
	       Should she **have said** something?
	—Yes, she **should have.**
		What **would** you **have done**?
		       Would you **have apologized**?
		—No, I **wouldn't have.**

c Complete the conversations with *would have, should have,* or *shouldn't have.*

A: Guess what? I got a ticket for double-parking in front of the bank.
B: Well, it's your fault. You <u>¹ shouldn't have</u> parked there. It blocks traffic.
A: What ²_____ you _____ done?
B: I ³_____ parked in the parking lot. That's what you're supposed to do!

C: The service at the gas station is terrible. Last week, I had to wait fifteen minutes.
D: They ⁴_____ made you wait so long. You ⁵_____ asked to speak to the manager.
     That's what I ⁶_____ done.

d Read about the situations. Then make sentences about what the person *should(n't) have done* or what you *would(n't) have done.*

Example   Situation 1: *I would have made a salad.*

STICKY SITUATIONS

What would you have done?

"I prepared an elaborate beef lasagna for my boss and his wife. An hour before they arrived, I remembered that she was a vegetarian."
–Barbara L., Dallas

"My girlfriend and I had tickets to a show. The night we were supposed to go, my boss asked me to work late on a special project, so we couldn't go. My girlfriend was furious."
–Robert S., Chicago

"I gave my brother a blue sweater for his birthday. A few months later, I noticed that my brother gave my father the exact same sweater for <u>his</u> birthday."
–Emilie P., Montreal

10 ▶ Reading

a Read these haiku (short poems) and answer the questions.

1 What problem are the poems about?
2 How does the writer feel about the problem?

b Read the article quickly to find out…

1 why these poems were written.
2 where this happened.
3 who started the idea.

> Clinton Street
> autos
> honk, guzzle and
> burn away
> our crisp, clean
> spring days

> I hear in
> New York
> shortest distance
> in time is
> from green light
> to honk.

guzzle = to drink or use a lot of something quickly

The Power of Poetry

Aaron Naparstek knows the exact moment when the car horns pushed him over the edge and turned him into a poet. It wasn't just the constant noise outside his Brooklyn apartment window when he was trying to work from home. It was the sheer futility of it–that New Yorkers believe honking their horns can actually dissolve a traffic jam, the way some people think that the more times they push an elevator button, the sooner it will arrive.

The noise made him irritated. He couldn't concentrate. He got to the point where he could distinguish different taxi models just by the sound of their horns. Then one day a guy in a blue sedan just made him snap. "He was leaning on his horn," Naparstek said. "It wasn't just 'toot, toot.' It was 'Nnnnnnnnnnnnnnnnnnnnnnnnn!'"

Naparstek threw several eggs at the car. The furious honker got out of his car and threatened him. While the driver shouted, the line of cars that were stacked up for blocks all started to honk their horns.

Naparstek realized that the egg-throwing had added to the problem. So he tried a nonviolent approach. He wrote a series of haiku—three-line poems in the classic Japanese 5-7-5 syllable form—and taped them on lampposts along his street. He called them "honku."

Clinton Street traffic
a vast river of honking
raging through my head

Drivers couldn't read the poetry from the street, so Naparstek wasn't expecting much of a response. But then other honku started to appear–ones he hadn't written. Soon the lampposts were covered with 17-syllable poems, some printed out and some handwritten under his.

A community movement was born! In the tree-lined neighborhood, dog walkers and parents pushing babies in strollers could be seen wandering away from the lampposts, counting syllables on their fingers as they composed their own honku. Neighbors gathered at corners to talk about the problem. Pedestrians began to chastise drivers. Finally, the honku-generated publicity brought five police officers to hand out tickets for noise violations. "It may be," said Naparstek, "the country's only example where police and politicians responded to poetry."

c Work with a partner. Complete the summary with your own words. Then compare answers with another pair.

Aaron Naparstek worked ¹_____*from home*_____. He found he couldn't concentrate because of ²_*Car honking*_. One day he became very angry when ³_*a driver leaned on his horn*_. So he ⁴_*threw eggs at the car*_. The driver was ⁵_*furious*_ so Naparstek realized that ⁶_*he added to a problem*_. Instead he started to write ⁷_*poems/haiku*_, which he called honku, and he attached them to ⁸_*lamppost*_ in his neighborhood. Soon ⁹_*other people*_ joined in. Finally, the police came to the neighborhood to ¹⁰_*hand out tickets*_ and the noise was reduced.

d Find these words and expressions on page 85. Use the context to try to figure out what they mean. (1) = paragraph number.

pushed him over the edge (1)	made him snap (2)	strollers (6)
futility (1)	stacked up (3)	noise violations (6)

e What other situations do you know of where neighbors came together to solve a problem?

11 ▸ Vocabulary: Adjectives that describe feelings

a Match the beginnings (1–9) with the endings (a–i) of the sentences.

1	Naparstek was **irritated**	1c	a	because his sister is more popular than he is.
2	He was **desperate**	7	b	because she has nobody to talk to.
3	The neighbors were **relieved**	9	c	by the noise outside his window.
4	They felt **proud**	8	d	for shouting at Pat. I shouldn't have done that.
5	The detectives are **confident**	4	e	of their success.
6	Thank you so much! I'm **grateful**	5	f	that they will find the criminal soon.
7	Kayla feels **lonely**	2	g	to make the drivers stop the noise.
8	I feel **guilty**	6	h	to you for all your help.
9	Andy is **jealous**	3	i	when the noise finally stopped.

b Which of the adjectives are usually positive or pleasant? Which ones are unpleasant?

c Work with a partner. Choose three of the words. Describe a time when you felt that way.

12 ▸ Writing

a Read this haiku. How does the writer feel?

b Choose an adjective from section 11. Write a haiku about it. Follow the guidelines for haiku. (*Line 1*: 5 syllables, *Line 2*: 7 syllables, *Line 3*: 5 syllables)

c Work in small groups. Read each other's poems. Which feeling is being described?

You see that painting
the one they're all
looking at
My son did that one

11 Make or break

✔ Justice and life decisions
✔ Third conditional; *whatever, wherever, whoever, whenever*

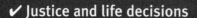

1 ▶ Reading

a Look at the picture. Identify the diamond and the excavator. What do you think is happening?

b Read the newspaper article quickly, and check the best title.
___ Priceless Diamond Stolen in London
___ Extra Police Ordered to Protect Giant Diamond
___ The Robbery That Never Was

c Read the article again. Write questions for the answers. Sometimes more than one question is possible.

1 London.
Where did this happen? / What city was the diamond in?

2 An excavator.
What were the men driving?
_____

3 They were going to steal the diamond.
_____
_____

4 They surrounded the thieves and arrested them.
_____
_____

5 Because the gang had been in a similar crime earlier.
_____
_____

6 Because they wanted to catch the thieves in the act.
_____
_____

7 No. It was a copy.
_____
_____

The tourists strolling around London's Millennium Dome thought they were in a James Bond movie. Crashing into the dome at high speed, men in gas masks were speeding towards them on an excavator, heading straight for the priceless Millennium Star diamond.

But the robbery ended almost as soon as it began. Just as the thieves were reaching in to grab their prize, armed police officers dressed as cleaners surrounded them and shouted at them to raise their hands. Two robbers were trapped inside. Four others were arrested outside the dome.

If the robbers had succeeded, the robbery would have been the biggest in the world. But the gang was already under suspicion following a similar raid a few months before. Then two of the men were spotted at the dome, investigating the jewel vault. Detectives guessed that they were planning to snatch the millennium diamond. Hundreds of plain-clothes police officers were sent to the dome to wait for the gang to strike.

It was important to arrest the men at the scene because if the police had arrested the thieves before the robbery actually began, they might not have had enough evidence to convict them. But even if the robbers had managed to pull it off, they would have been disappointed. The real millennium star diamond had been replaced by a copy…just in case.

d Find these verbs in the article. Use the context to try to figure out what they mean. (1) = paragraph number.

speeding (1) trapped (2) strike (3)
grab (2) snatch (3)

▼ Help Desk

You **steal** money or things, but you **rob** a person or a place.

Thieves **robbed** the bank and **stole** five thousand dollars.

e What do you think? Did the police do the right thing? Why (not)?

2 Focus on Grammar

a Look at the sentence from the article. Then circle the correct responses in questions 1 and 2.

If the robbers had succeeded, the robbery would have been the biggest in the world.

1 The robbers (succeeded / didn't succeed).
2 This describes (a wish for the future / a hypothetical situation in the past).

b Look at the chart. What form of the verb is used in a) the *if* clause? b) the main clause?

Third conditional (past unreal conditions)	
If *clause*	***Main clause***
If the robbers **had succeeded,**	the raid **would have been** the biggest in the world.
If the police **hadn't surrounded** them,	the robbers **could have escaped.**
If the thieves **had escaped,**	the police **might not have had** enough evidence.
If you **had been there,**	what **would** you **have done?**

Note: The order of the clauses can be reversed.
*What would you have done **if you had been there?***

c Use the words in parentheses to make hypotheses about the robbery. Use *might*, *would*, or *could* in the main clause.

1 If the robbers _____had stolen_____ (steal) the diamond, the robbery _____ (break) the world record.
2 If the police _____ (be) in uniform, the tourists _____ (notice) them.
3 If the tourists _____ (know) about the robbery, they _____ (not visit) the Dome.
4 The raid _____ (succeed) if the robbers _____ (plan) it differently.
5 The police _____ (not suspect) the gang if they _____ (not be) under suspicion for a similar robbery a few months before.
6 Even if the gang _____ (get away), they _____ (not take) the real diamond.

d Make sentences about your own life. Then compare your answers with a partner.

1 If I (had / hadn't) _____, I (would / wouldn't) have _____.
2 If I (had / hadn't) _____, I (could / couldn't) have _____.
3 If I (had / hadn't) _____, I (might / might not) have _____.

3 ▶ Vocabulary: Crime

a Look at the newspaper headlines. Underline the words that describe crimes. Then find which words fit the definitions below.

1 attacking and robbing someone in a public place: *mugging*

2 the crime of damaging property on purpose: *vandalism*

3 using a computer to access private information on another computer: *hacking*

4 the crime of threatening to tell a secret if someone doesn't do what you want: *blackmail*

5 stealing from a store: *shoplifting*

Vandalism on the rise in public parks: Benches broken and painted

Rock star charged for shoplifting at department store

Man in hospital after mugging in public park

Company chief found guilty of blackmail: Threatened to tell employees about boss's criminal past

Teenager arrested for hacking into police computer system

b Put the sentences in a logical order. Then discuss the meaning of the words in bold with a partner.

3 Several **witnesses** came and described what they saw at the scene of the crime.

2 His **trial** was last week. At the trial, he appeared before a **judge** and a **jury**.

6 The judge **sentenced** him to nine months in prison and a **fine** of five thousand dollars.

1 The suspect was **arrested** and **charged with** shoplifting.

5 They decided he was guilty and **convicted** him.

4 The jury listened carefully to the **evidence** from the witnesses.

c **AUDIO** Listen and check your answers. Repeat the sentences.

d Describe a crime or a court case that has been in the news recently. Use as many of the words in 3a and 3b as you can.

4 ▶ *KnowHow*: Linking

a **AUDIO** Listen and repeat the expressions. Pay attention to how the words are linked.

experienced criminal   Best Bank   back door   alert customer   pleaded guilty

b **AUDIO** Now listen and repeat the story. Practice linking the consonants.

Jack was an **experienced criminal**. He **robbed banks**.

Last June he entered Best Bank through the **back door**.

He **walked calmly** to the **bank teller**.

An **alert customer** called the police. They **arrested Jack**.

Jack **pleaded guilty**. He **spent time** in a **dark jail**.

5 ▶ Listening

a What does this expression mean: "The punishment should fit the crime"?

b **AUDIO** Listen. Jeannie and Lyle are talking about unusual punishments. What three punishments do they describe?

c **AUDIO** Listen again. For each punishment, choose the statement that Jeannie and Lyle both agree on.

    1 a The punishment probably helped the young people understand how their neighbors felt.
       b The punishment wasn't very effective.
    2 a The punishment was too light. The landlord should have gone to prison.
       b The punishment was practical as well as effective.
    3 a Jeannie and her friend learned a lesson from the punishment.
       b They learned to love gym class.

d What other "punishments that fit the crime" have you heard of?

6 ▶ Speaking

a Work in small groups. Each person chooses a different case from the list below. What would you need to know in order to decide on an appropriate punishment for this person? Think of at least three questions you would ask.

    Example A child who wrote graffiti on the outside wall of his or her school *How old was the child? Had he or she done this before? Were other children involved? What did the graffiti say?*

    1 Someone who got on a bus without paying the fare
    2 Someone who promised to take care of a friend's garden while the friend was away, but then forgot to do it
    3 A computer student who hacked into his or her university's computer system
    4 Someone who made long-distance calls on someone else's phone
    5 A teenager who lied about his or her age to get into a movie

b Individually, answer your questions and develop a story about the case.

    Example *A twelve-year-old girl wrote graffiti because her older friend persuaded her to. She had never been in trouble before. The graffiti said "AK loves BJ."*

c Present the case to the group. As a group, decide on an appropriate punishment for each case.

7 ▶ Reading

a Work with a partner. Discuss the questions.

1 How can the people you know influence the choices you make in your life?
2 How important is it to meet the right people at certain times?

b Read the article quickly. Find five ways in which Doug influenced Rudy's life.

Points of View

This week, Rudy Cox and Doug Peterson describe their relationship.

"I didn't want to let him down."

Rudy: I met Doug when I was sixteen. At the time, I had run away from home. I was staying with my cousin and hanging out with a rough crowd of kids. I didn't know what I wanted to do with my life. I was just into skateboarding and drawing cartoons.

I only applied for a scholarship to get into college because I didn't know what else to do. I had an interview with Doug. I was amazed that this important professor was taking an interest in me. Even though I didn't get the scholarship, he encouraged me to apply to college anyway. He took me through the application process, showed me how to apply for financial aid, and helped me find a place to live.

Doug continued to watch out for me all through college. I probably would have dropped out, if it hadn't been for him. He kept on asking me about my grades, especially when they were low! So I stayed in school. I didn't want to let him down because I had so much respect for him. Over the years, he became like a father to me.

It was Doug who suggested that I put together a comic strip for the college newspaper. So I did that, and it was pretty successful. Then Doug put me in touch with an ex-student of his, Paul, who was a successful cartoonist. Paul really liked my work, but he advised me to get some computer skills. So I taught myself everything I could about using the computer for design. After I graduated, I looked for work in advertising and design.

Now I'm an art director for an entertainment network. It's a great job. Sometimes I wake up in the morning and say, "How did I get here?" I know it's mainly because of Doug. If I hadn't met him, I probably would have gotten on the wrong track.

"He's like a son."

Doug: I first met Rudy when he applied for a scholarship program at the university where I teach. He was very unsure of himself. It was hard to get him to talk about himself at all. But it was obvious that he was intelligent. He was an athlete, too. He used to scare the wits out of me sliding down steps and banisters on a skateboard, so one of the first things I did was to take him to a sports store where he could get a helmet.

It was clear that he needed help figuring out how to get into college, how to get housing, and all that. He didn't have a clue. I helped him and kept an eye on him.

I felt he needed something to give him some focus, so I suggested that he do the comic strip for the student newspaper. He had done something like that in high school. He was very good at it. The strip won a couple of national awards. Then he realized that he had enough talent to do design work for a living and that was what he wanted to do. I supported him in his decision. It was hard at first. My wife and I had to put him up every now and again when he couldn't afford a place to live. But he didn't give up, and now he's very successful.

Rudy is like a son to us. I drop by his office whenever I go into the city. We have lunch, and he tells me what he's doing. I'm glad that things have turned out so well for him.

c Underline the following sentences in the article on page 91. Use the context to try to figure out what the underlined expressions mean. (1) = paragraph number.

1 I <u>was</u> just <u>into</u> skateboarding and drawing cartoons. (1)
2 I probably would have <u>gotten on the wrong track</u>. (5)
3 He used to <u>scare the wits out of</u> me. (6)
4 I helped him and <u>kept an eye on</u> him. (7)

d Work with a partner. Discuss the questions.

1 What do you think was the most important thing that Doug did for Rudy?
2 Who do you think has the greater influence on young people—friends or family?

8 ▶ Vocabulary: Phrasal verbs

a Match the phrasal verbs (1–9) on the left with a definition on the right (a–i). (All of the verbs are in the article on page 91.)

1	hang out	1f	a assemble or create something
2	drop out	2g	b visit a place informally
3	keep on	3i	c find an answer to a problem
4	let down	4e	d stop doing something
5	put together	5a	e make someone disappointed in you
6	figure out	6c	f spend time in a place, not doing very much
7	put up	7h	g stop attending school or a university
8	give up	8d	h give someone a place to stay
9	drop by	9b	i continue doing something

b Fill in the blanks with one of the phrasal verbs above.

1 We haven't seen you for ages. Why don't you ___drop by___ for a cup of coffee?
2 Nobody expected Judy to finish the marathon, but she just _keep on_ running!
3 Teenagers in my neighborhood like to _hang out_ at the park.
4 My brother never finished college. He _dropped out_ after a year and became a chef.
5 We couldn't finish the crossword puzzle, so we _gave up_ and looked at the answers.
6 We don't know what's wrong with our car. The mechanic is trying to _put_ it _together_.
7 I'm depending on you to help me. Please don't _let_ me _down_.
8 The parents have _figured out_ a plan to improve our local school.
9 My sister doesn't have a place to live, so we're going to _put_ her _up_ for a while.

> ▼ **Help Desk**
>
> When *let down, give up, put together, figure out,* and *put up* are used with an object pronoun, the pronoun goes between the verb and the particle.
>
> *Don't let me down.* (Not: ~~Don't let down me.~~)

c Choose four of the verbs above that are most useful to you. Write sentences to help you remember them.

9 ▶ Listening

a AUDIO Listen to people describing advice that they received. Complete the chart.

Speaker	What was the advice?	Who gave it?
1		
2		
3		
4		

b AUDIO Listen again. Why was each piece of advice useful, according to the speakers?

c Work with a partner. Describe a time when someone gave you good advice. What did the person say, and why was it useful?

10 ▶ Focus on Grammar

a Look at the chart. Choose *a* or *b*.

1 *Whatever, wherever, whoever, whenever* mean…
   a any, or no matter which thing, place, person, or time.
   b a specific thing, place, person, or time.
2 When the sentence refers to the future, use __ after *whatever, wherever, whoever,* or *whenever*.
   a a present form   b a future form

Whatever, wherever, whoever, whenever

Whenever she has a problem that she can't work out, she goes for a walk.
I'll give this package to **whoever answers the door**.
You can go **wherever you like**, as long as you stay inside the building.
Whatever you do, always check a mirror before you go out.
Whoever you talk to, just ask questions.

---

b Fill in the blanks with *whatever, wherever, whoever,* or *whenever*.

1 __*Whenever*__ I call Vanessa, she says she's busy.
2 We can do _____ you like. I don't mind.
3 Please sit down _____ you can find a seat.
4 _____ told you to park here was wrong.
5 _____ happens, I'll never forget you.
6 _____ he is, the police will find him.

c Finish the sentences with your own information.

1 I get together with my friends whenever _____.
2 When I'm at a party, I talk to whoever _____.
3 This weekend I'll probably do whatever _____.
4 When I was a child, I played wherever _____.

11 ▶ Language in Action: Gratitude

a AUDIO Why did Helga win the tournament? Listen to the interview.

b AUDIO Listen again and complete the conversation. Then check your answers with the chart.

Interviewer: So it all turned out OK.

Helga: Yes, it did. I think it's ¹_____ the break that I played so well this season.

Interviewer: You had a new coach, too, right?

Helga: Yes, and I ²_____ to her. I ³_____ done it if she ⁴_____ pushed so hard.

EXPRESSING GRATITUDE

- I'm grateful to (person).
- I owe a lot to (person).
- If it weren't for…, I wouldn't have….
- It's because of…that I….
- I wouldn't / couldn't have… if (person) hadn't….

---

c Work with a partner. A, you are a journalist. B, you are one of the two people described below. Express gratitude to the people who helped you. Use the expressions in the chart.

Example A: *Congratulations on… How do you feel?*
B: *I feel great! But I owe a lot to…*

Russell Loy
Best New Singer award
Thanks family, friends, manager

Pamela Finlay
Climbed Mt. Everest
Thanks team members, husband

12 ▶ Speaking and Writing

a Choose one of the following topics:

**an event that affected your life   an experience that taught you something
a decision that you made that turned out OK**

b Work with a partner. A, describe…

1 where and when the experience happened.
2 what exactly happened—what you thought, how you felt, and what people said.
3 how you feel about it now—what changed and how things might have been different.

B, listen and ask questions if necessary.

c Write a short composition describing your experience. Write three paragraphs.

d Exchange papers with a new partner. How were your experiences similar? How were they different?

12 A laugh a day

✔ Health and laughter
✔ Structures with *there + be*; connectors

1 ▶ Reading

a Look at the picture and the title of the article. What do you think "Musicians on Call" does?

b Read the article quickly. Make notes under the headings with the most important information from the article.

Who?	Where?	What?	Why?
Vivek Tiwary and Michael Solomon			

Musicians ON Call

VIVEK TIWARY AND MICHAEL SOLOMON had each lost loved ones to serious illness, so they had both spent plenty of hours in grim hospital settings. They were determined to make something positive come out of the experience. The inspiration came when the friends, both involved in the music business, were helping arrange music performances at a local hospital.

One night, a nurse approached them and explained that some patients were too sick to come to the lounge where the performances were being held. She asked whether one of the performers could do a song or two in a patient's room. "It was a magical moment," recalls Tiwary. "The one-to-one interaction between the musician and the people in the [hospital] community had a very powerful effect."

Solomon and Tiwary were aware that studies have shown that music helps in pain management and healing, but this first-hand experience gave them real proof of the benefits. So they designed a plan that would bring performers to the hospital at designated times to

go from room to room and perform for any patient who wanted to hear them. They named it Musicians on Call (MOC).

MOC's mission is "to use music and entertainment to complement the healing process and to improve the quality of life for patients." Solomon and Tiwary used their connections to the music business to raise money. Bruce Springsteen donated several rows of tickets and backstage passes to be sold online. Britney Spears, the Who, Def Leppard, and the Black Crowes have also supported the cause.

However, it is regular artists, rather than big names, who volunteer for in-hospital performances, workshops, and lessons. Music instruction is a big part of MOC's mission, but for some patients, just listening to music can be comforting. "The air changes in the room," says Solomon. Tiwary adds, "It has nothing to do with how you look, who you are, who wrote the song…if you can make music, there's a patient whose day you can brighten."

Solomon calls MOC "the most meaningful thing I've ever done," and now has an even larger goal. He says, "Every hospital in the world will have this program before I die if I can help it."

c Read the article again. Complete the sentences.

1 Tiwary and Solomon started *Musicians on Call* because <u>they wanted to bring music to patients</u>.
2 They got the idea when _____.
3 Their first experience of a musician playing for a patient showed them that

   _____.
4 They were able to raise money by _____.
5 In addition to playing for patients, MOC also _____.
6 Solomon would like to _____.

d Find these words in the article. Use the context to try to figure out what they mean.
(1) = paragraph number.

   grim (1)   lounge (2)   healing (3)   first-hand (3)   donated (4)   brighten (5)

e What do you think of MOC? Have you ever heard of anything like this?

2 ▶ Vocabulary: Sickness and health

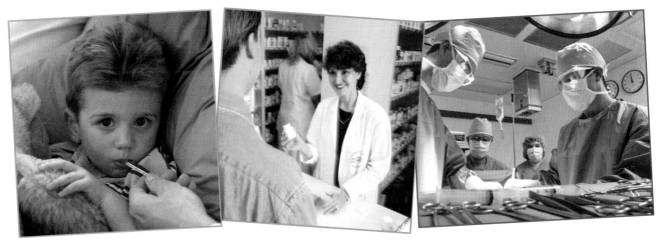

a Answer the questions using the words below.

   vaccine   antibiotic   pharmacy   fever   flu (influenza)
   headache   measles   aspirin   surgeon

1 What are two common **contagious diseases**?   *flu and* _____
2 What are two common **symptoms** of **flu** (influenza)?   _____
3 What kind of medication is **penicillin**?   _____
4 What kind of doctor performs an **operation**?   _____
5 What **medication** might you take if you have a headache? _____
6 Where do you fill a **prescription**?   _____
7 What protects people against **contagious diseases**?   _____

b Put the words from 2a in the chart below. Then add words from the article in section 1.

Illness or symptom	Treatment	Hospital

3 ▶ In Conversation

AUDIO What kind of programs is Doctor Levy describing? Listen. Then read.

Interviewer: Doctor Levy, tell us about some of the more unusual services here at the hospital.

Doctor: Well, we have yoga classes, art, and music programs. And starting next month, there's going to be a comedy night every Friday.

Interviewer: Really? Why comedy?

Doctor: Well, there's been quite a lot of research to suggest that laughter speeds up the healing process.

Interviewer: That sounds wonderful. Are other hospitals starting programs like yours?

Doctor: Well, some, yes. And I think there should be programs like this in every hospital.

4 ▶ Focus on Grammar

a Underline the subject of each sentence in the chart. Then answer questions 1 and 2.

1 Which subjects are singular and which are plural?
2 How does this affect the verb in the first four sentences?

Structures with *there* + *be*

There	is going to be	a comedy night every Friday.
	are going to be	some unusual services at the hospital.
	has been	quite a lot of research into this.
	have been	many changes in health care.
	should be	programs like this in every hospital.
	used to be	a hospital here, but it closed.

Note: *There is* and *there has* can both be contracted to *there's*.

b Fill in the blanks, using a structure with *there* + *be* and the word in parentheses.

1 In the future, ____*there will be*____ (will) more music in hospitals.
2 _____ (should) a hospital in this area.
3 _____ (used to) more family doctors than there are now.
4 The doctor says _____ (might) a better medication available next year.
5 As the population gets older, _____ (going to) a need for more nursing homes.
6 _____ (have) several cases of malaria recently. _____ (must) a reason for this.

c Work with a partner. Use structures with *there* + *be* to make sentences about the following topics. Add your own ideas.

Example   *There is going to be a new hospital in my city. There should be better health care.*

enough doctors	more technology	unusual treatments
cheaper medication	a cure for diseases	better health care

5 ▶ Language in Action: Information about health

a AUDIO Match the conversations (1–3) you hear with the pictures.

b AUDIO Listen again. Write 1, 2, or 3 next to the expressions that are used in each conversation. 1 = conversation number.

GIVING INFORMATION	RESPONDING TO INFORMATION
___ I don't feel very well.	___ Oh dear.
___ I'm coming down with something.	___ Why don't you…?
___ She's a bit run down.	___ I hope you feel better.
___ She's not very well.	___ I hope it's nothing serious.
___ She's feeling much better.	___ Give (name) my best wishes.
___ She'll be back at work soon.	___ I'm glad to hear that.

c Work with a partner. Practice your own conversations for the situations in 5a. Use the expressions in the chart.

6 ▶ Speaking

a Work in groups. Discuss how each factor can have a positive and / or negative effect on health.

diet   exercise   work   family   personality   interests and hobbies

Example   *Diet can have a positive effect on health if you eat healthy food like fruit and vegetables. It can have a negative effect if there is too much fat and sugar in your diet.*

b Discuss the questions.

1   Which three factors do you think have the greatest effect on health?
2   Think of advice that you would give someone for a healthy life.

7 ▶ Listening

a Look at the picture. What do you think the purpose of a laughter club might be?

b **AUDIO** Listen to the interview and number the topics in order.

___ how to set up a laughter club
___ how laughter clubs began
___ what happens in a laughter club
___ the benefits of laughter

c **AUDIO** Listen again. Write T (true) or F (false), according to the interview.

1 Laughter clubs are an American invention. ___
2 Laughter relieves stress. ___
3 The purpose of the clubs is to help people make friends. ___
4 You can be trained to be a laughter club leader. ___
5 People tell a lot of jokes in laughter clubs. ___
6 Sometimes people laugh because they see others laughing. ___

d Would you join a laughter club? Why or why not?

8 ▶ Vocabulary: Three-word verbs

a What do the expressions mean? Choose the correct definition.

1 A doctor named Madan Kataria <u>came up with the idea</u>.
  a brought the idea to America   b thought of the idea
2 They used to tell jokes, but they <u>ran out of jokes</u>, so now they don't use them.
  a couldn't think of any more jokes   b had too many jokes

b Underline the three-word verbs in the conversation. Then match each verb with a definition.

Dave: Let's go swimming!
Liana: I can't. I have a class at three o'clock, and I can't get out of it.
Dave: Can't you say that you're sick, or something?
Liana: I'd never get away with that. Everybody uses that excuse. Anyway, I have a lot of work to do if I want to keep up with the rest of the class. I still have to make up for the time I was absent last week.
Dave: I think you should cut down on the number of classes you're taking. You're working too hard.

1 do something wrong without being punished for it   *get away with*
2 move at the same speed as   _____
3 avoid doing something that you have promised to do   _____
4 reduce   _____
5 do something that corrects a bad situation   _____

c Write sentences using the verbs above. Then erase the verbs and ask a partner to put them back in.

9 ▶ Reading

a Look at the pictures. Which of these situations do you find funny? Why do you think some people laugh at these situations?

b Read the article. What are three reasons why we laugh?

WHY DO WE LAUGH?

Why do we laugh? To understand what is involved in humor, let us examine how some psychologists explain it.

Some psychologists believe that humor is related to superiority. Plato, for example, believed that whenever something or someone is degraded, we laugh because we feel superior. Similarly, when a person slips on a banana peel, we laugh because of our superiority over the situation. Other examples of this kind of humor include caricatures that make someone look comical or ugly.

Another reason we laugh is that we see incongruity: two things side by side that do not normally belong together. An example of verbal incongruity might be a joke where the person is expecting to hear one outcome, but is surprised by a different one. Incongruity can be found in visual humor as well. For example, The famous comic duo, Laurel and Hardy, made people laugh because one of them was very fat and the other was very thin. Visual forms of incongruity are among the most humorous. Thus, cartoons without any captions are often the most humorous of all, because they rely on visual incongruity.

However, these aren't the only reasons we laugh. One theory suggests that laughter is a reaction to a potentially difficult or embarrassing situation. Humor helps us to deal with stress caused by embarrassment. Similarly, people laugh when something is so unexpected or taboo that it shocks their senses. For this reason, audiences sometimes laugh at violence in comedy shows. ■

c Read the article again. Complete the chart.

Why do we laugh?		
Reason	Example	Picture
1 *to feel superior*	*caricatures,*	
2		
3		

d Which explanation do you prefer?

Focus on Grammar

a Use connectors to make logical connections between sentences. Look at the chart below. Then underline the connectors in the article in section 9. Where do connectors usually go in a sentence?

Connectors	
Addition	also, in addition, besides
Sequence	first, second, next, then, finally
Example	for example
Result	as a result, therefore, thus
Reason	because of this, for this reason
Similarity	similarly, in the same way
Contrast	however, nevertheless, on the other hand

 **Help Desk**

Begin a new sentence when using connectors. *Stan Laurel was thin. However, Oliver Hardy was fat.* (Not: ~~Stan Laurel was thin, however, Oliver Hardy was fat.~~)

b Circle the most appropriate connectors.

Laughter often occurs in a relaxed context. ¹ (Nevertheless / For example), when a parent or other familiar person tickles a small child, it makes the child laugh. ² (In addition / On the other hand), most young children will not laugh, and may even cry, when tickled by a stranger. ³ (As a result / Similarly), they will be frightened by someone's sudden appearance if they are not expecting it. ⁴ (Because of this / Finally), scientists have concluded that people laugh when they are in a playful mood and are comfortable in their surroundings.

KnowHow: English outside the classroom

a Read the paragraph. How does this student's hobby help him learn more English?

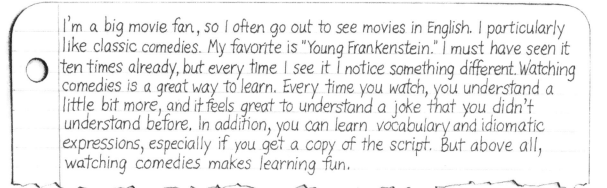

I'm a big movie fan, so I often go out to see movies in English. I particularly like classic comedies. My favorite is "Young Frankenstein." I must have seen it ten times already, but every time I see it I notice something different. Watching comedies is a great way to learn. Every time you watch, you understand a little bit more, and it feels great to understand a joke that you didn't understand before. In addition, you can learn vocabulary and idiomatic expressions, especially if you get a copy of the script. But above all, watching comedies makes learning fun.

b Work in small groups. Think of some other interesting ways to improve your English outside the classroom. Add to the chart.

Ways to practice speaking and listening	Ways to practice reading and writing
English movies	Magazines and newspapers in English
English conversation groups or clubs	

c What is your favorite way to learn English outside the classroom?

12 ▶ Writing

a Use your ideas from section 11 to write two paragraphs about learning English outside the classroom. Answer the questions below. Use connectors to link your ideas.

Paragraph 1:   What are some popular ways to learn English outside the classroom?
                     What are the advantages and disadvantages of these methods?
Paragraph 2:   What is your favorite way to learn English outside the classroom and why?

b Work in small groups. Read each others' paragraphs. Whose method is the most unusual?

13 ▶ Listening and Speaking

a `AUDIO` Listen to the jokes. As you listen, choose an appropriate ending (punch line) for each joke. Write the number of the joke next to each punch line.

__ "It doesn't work, does it?"
__ "I'm afraid you don't know much about my father, sir."
__ "Now run as fast as you can!"

b `AUDIO` Listen to the jokes from 13a with the punch lines to check your answers.

c Work with a partner. Practice telling the jokes. Use the words and expressions below to help you.

1   borrow / pay back / "How much will he owe me?"
2   my grandfather / door bell / "Let me do it!"
3   cream / "What's that for?" / wipe off

d Work in groups. Tell a joke that you know.

> ▼ **Help Desk**
>
> The present tense is often used to tell a joke or a story to make it more dramatic.
>
> *The teacher **is trying** to teach some basic math, so he **says** to a little boy....*

14 ▶ Listening: Song

a `AUDIO` Listen to the song. Check the words you hear. (You will hear some words more than once.)

__ looking   __ laughing   __ sighing   __ rain
__ smiling   __ keep on   __ shining   __ sun
__ bring on   __ crying   __ put on   __ clouds

b `AUDIO` Listen to the song again. Use the words to help you write the lyrics line by line.

c `AUDIO` Listen again. Check your answers. What is the message of this song?

Grammar

1 Read the article. How would most robbers have behaved? What did the robber imagine?

MAY I ROB YOU, PLEASE?

A gray-haired robber went into a shop, smiled at the clerk, and explained that his company had gone bankrupt. He politely asked her if he could have the money in the cash register, and then he apologized. He escaped with $200.

Robbery is a crime even if you are polite. But if the robber had threatened the clerk, the incident would have seemed much worse. Why? Some people say that having good manners is simply imagining how another person feels. This robber imagined how he would have felt if someone had violently demanded money from him or threatened his life. Whatever you might think of his behavior, there is a lesson in his actions that we can carry into our everyday lives. So, be polite, but don't rob a bank!

2 The clerk reported the robbery to the police. Complete her statements.

1 The robber told me _his company had gone bankrupt._ ("My company has gone bankrupt.")

2 He asked _____. ("Can I have the contents of the cash register?")

3 He said _____. ("I'm sorry.")

4 I said _____. ("I've been robbed by the nicest robber in town!")

3 Combine the sentences to form a sentence in the third conditional.

1 The jokes weren't very funny. She didn't tell them well. _The jokes would have been funny if she had told them well._

2 I didn't remember his name. I felt embarrassed.

_____

3 They didn't come to the performance. They worked late.

_____

4 He lost his job. He robbed the store as a result.

_____

5 I got ill very often. I didn't eat well.

_____

6 I wanted to apologize to her. I didn't have the chance.

_____

4 Circle the correct word or phrase.

1 (What / Whatever) Tamara does, it is always done with good taste and manners.

2 We can go wherever you (want / will want) tomorrow. I'm open to suggestions.

3 (They / There) are going to be three comedians at the Comedy Club this evening.

4 (Who / Whoever) told you to eat more salt doesn't know much about nutrition.

5 There (has / is) been a huge increase in the use of new treatments in this hospital.

6 Whatever you (do / did), put gas in the car before you leave.

7 He always makes friends easily wherever (does he go / he goes).

8 There is a problem with my arm. It hurts whenever I (will move / move) it.

5 Fill in the blanks with the connectors from the list.

for example	finally
because of this	in the same way
on the other hand	as a result

Dear Editor,

I believe that some people are not teaching their children good manners.
¹ *For example*, many people don't teach their kids to say thank you for gifts or favors. ² _____, children don't learn the value of what others do for them.
³ _____, we don't teach them to respect the property of others.
⁴ _____, they are careless of their own and others' property. ⁵ _____, young people who are brought up well show respect and understanding.
⁶ _____, I would like to say that the best way to teach manners is by example.

Yours,
Lydia Walters

Vocabulary

6 Fill in the correct words. Use the first letters to help you.

1 Kristi is j*ealous* because her best friend has a boyfriend and she doesn't.
2 If you go to the pharmacy, could you get this p_____ filled for me?
3 Because there was not enough evidence, the j_____ could not decide if the suspect was g_____.
4 After the o_____ was over, the surgeon came and told us that Tina was OK.
5 You feel warm. Do you have a f_____?
6 The judged sentenced the criminal to five years in prison and a f_____ of $10,000 for h_____ into a government computer system.

7 Complete the sentences with the missing parts of the three-word verbs.

1 She *came* _up_ _with_ a great idea for solving the problem.
2 When the hospital *ran* ____ ____ the medication, they had to wait for more.
3 You promised to help, and now you can't *get* ____ ____ it.
4 I wish you'd *cut* ____ ____ the amount of sugar you eat. It's way too much!
5 I couldn't *keep* ____ ____ the others in the race so I came in last.
6 He'll never *get* ____ ____ that. Someone will find out and punish him.

Recycling Center

8 Combine the sentences using a relative clause. Omit the relative pronoun (*who, which, that*) when possible.

1 He is the criminal. He stole half a million dollars. *He is the criminal who stole half a million dollars.*
2 That's the video. I told you about it.

   _____

3 She's the woman. She knew my grandmother.

   _____

4 This is a book. I'll never forget it.

   _____

5 Tara Jones is the surgeon. She operated on Kimberly.

   _____

Fun Spot

Read the haiku. Unscramble the underlined letters to find out how this person feels. Unscramble the circled letters to find out what the gift is.

The gift is perfect
I will use it every day
Thank you very much

Keep on talking!

UNIT 1 ▸ Communicating without words: Student A

(For **B**'s part of this activity, go to page 107.)

1 Work with a partner. **A**, You are a guest at a hotel. Choose one of the messages. Without using any words, try to make your partner understand what the message says. You can use hand gestures, body language, and drawings, but you must not speak or write words. Your partner will guess the message.

I don't have hot water.	**Wake me up at 9:00 a.m.**
What time did my friend call?	**Where is the restaurant?**

2 After your partner guesses correctly, change roles. If your partner can't guess after five tries, tell your partner what the message is. Take turns, and do as many messages as you can.

UNIT 2 ▸ Creative careers!

1 Work with a partner. **A**, choose a "creative career" that you are interested in. **B**, use the expressions below to help you think of questions to ask your partner about the career. Take notes.

> **been in**
> **interested in**
> **good at**
> **thought about**

2 Change roles. When both of you have information about your partner's "creative career," present your partner's information to the class.

3 Now compare answers with the class. Categorize the types of careers chosen in the chart. Which category are the most people interested in?

Performers	Athletes	Writers
Paula–ballet dancer	Larry–golfer	Cecilia–poet

UNIT 3 Are you connected?

1 Write your answers in the chart.

	Your Answer	Others
A country you've been to		
The year you started studying English		
The city you were born in		
Your middle name		
An aunt's name		
Number of brothers		
Something you've had repaired recently		
What you had for lunch yesterday		

2 Now ask questions to find other people that have the same answer as you do. Put a check mark in the chart above for each person you find.

Example   *Have you been to Italy?*   –*Yes, I have.*
                When did you start studying English?   –*1995.*

A country you've been to	*Italy*	√√√√
The year you started studying English	*2002*	

3 Compare your results with the class. For which items did you find the most people that shared your answer?

UNIT 4 Job descriptions

1 Work with a partner. Discuss the jobs and job duties in the chart. Which duties fit each job? Several of the duties may apply to more than one job.

2 Work with another pair. Compare answers. Which job do you think is the most difficult?

3 Choose one of the jobs. Create a job description. Add at least two more duties that are not in the chart.

JOBS:

ACCOUNTANT · COMPUTER PROGRAMMER OFFICE ADMINISTRATOR · SALESPERSON

Duties:

- Answer telephones.
- Attend meetings.
- Be courteous.
- Be prompt.
- Make phone calls.
- Meet with clients.
- Read reports.

- Report to supervisor(s).
- Schedule meetings.
- Sell new products.
- Supervise other employees.
- Take messages.
- Test software.

- Travel.
- Type reports.
- Work with a team.
- Work with computers.
- Write letters.
- Write new software.
- Write reports.

UNIT
1 ▶ Communicating without words: Student B

(For A's part of this activity, go to page 105.)

1 Work with a partner. **B**, you are a receptionist at a hotel. Without using any words, your partner will try to make you understand a message. Guess the message.

2 After you guess correctly, change roles. If your partner can't guess after five tries, tell your partner what the message is. Take turns, and do as many messages as you can.

Call me at 7:00 a.m.   **Where is the swimming pool?**
Which floor is my room on?   **I lost my key.**

UNIT
5 ▶ Helping out

1 Work in small groups. Look at the advertisement. Follow the four-step guidelines.

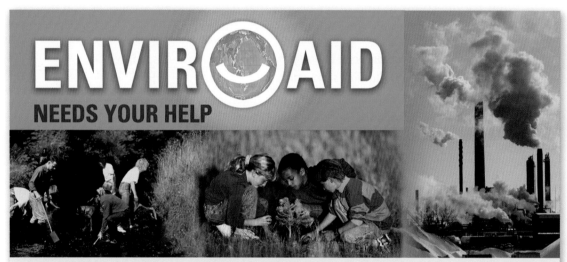

ENVIROAID
NEEDS YOUR HELP

Enviro-Aid *is looking for groups who want to improve these situations. Make your community a better place to live.*

- overused parks   • water pollution   • air pollution
- trash   • overcrowded highways • polluted beaches

Follow the four-step guidelines below. Then contact us with an outline of your plan of action.

❶ *Decide which situation you would like to help with.*
❷ *Decide what kind of help you can give (money, publicity, time, etc.).*
❸ *Plan how you can get other people involved.*
❹ *Decide on the details (how much time/money you can give, when you can start, your exact goals).*

We'll help you make it work!
Contact: Rita Delillo, EAI headquarters, tel. 899-555-8888, e-mail: ridel@eai.kwh

2 Present your plan to the class. Whose plan do you think will have the best result? Which one is the most practical?

^{UNIT}
6 ▶ **Once upon a time**

1   Work in small groups. Use the list of characters to finish the folk tale. Decide together what will happen. Make notes.

> **Edward:**   older brother, very athletic but lazy, not very intelligent
> **Bella:**   older sister, very practical and intelligent, likes to tell others what to do
> **Damien:**   younger brother, very artistic, loves to read and write
> **Susan:**   younger sister, likes to play tricks on others, loves adventures

> ONCE UPON A TIME there were two brothers and two sisters. They lived with their father in a big house in the countryside. Their father was very rich, and none of them ever had to do any work. But one day when they woke up they found that their father had disappeared, and with him all of their money.
> "We must find Father right away!" Edward, the older brother, said.
> "We must learn how to take care of ourselves!" Bella, the older sister, said.
> Damien and Susan, the younger brother and sister, looked at each other and started to cry.

2   Share your folk tales with the class. Which are the most interesting? Why? Do any of them teach a lesson?

^{UNIT}
7 ▶ **Zoom, zoom: Student A**

(For **B**'s part of this activity, go to page 110.)

1   Work with a partner. **A**, ask your partner questions to complete the first paragraph in the article. Use the question words in parentheses to help you.

2   Now answer **B**'s questions about the second paragraph. The answers are underlined.

The Human Transport (HT) was invented by
¹_____ (who). It was designed to move with
²_____ (what). It goes forward when the
body moves forward. It can also go backward. It is powered
³_____ (how). It is good for the environment
because ⁴_____ (why). The public was told
about the invention on ⁵_____ (when).

The HT became available for purchase on <u>November 18th, 2002</u>. You have to <u>take a training class</u> before you can drive it. You can carry packages on it, but not passengers. It travels <u>up to 12.5 miles per hour</u>. It doesn't have brakes because <u>the speed is controlled by your movement</u>. It can be used <u>indoors or outdoors</u>. It can be driven on roads or even grass!

3   Work in small groups. What do you think are the advantages of the HT? What are the disadvantages?

UNIT 8 ▶ Service survey

1   Complete the questionnaire.

QUESTIONNAIRE

Please take a moment to complete this questionnaire. Thank you.

- **TV**
- **radio**
- **outside advertising**
  (bus stops, billboards)

- **magazines**
- **newspapers**
- **Internet**

1   Which three of the above kinds of advertising do you encounter most often?
   _____   _____   _____

2   Which two of the above kinds of advertising do you pay the most attention to?
   _____   _____

3   Which two of the above kinds of advertising do you pay the least attention to?
   _____   _____

4   What two recent or current advertising campaigns do you think are particularly
   effective? _____   _____

2   Work in groups. Discuss your answers. Think of two pieces of advice that you would give
   to advertisers to make their advertising more effective.

Zoom, zoom: Student B

(For **A**'s part of this activity, go to page 108.)

1   Work with a partner. **B**, answer your partner's questions about the first paragraph in the article. The answers are underlined.

2   Now ask your partner questions to complete the second paragraph. Use the question words in parentheses to help you.

The Human Transport (HT) was invented by <u>Dean Kamen</u>. It was designed to move with <u>the human body</u>. It goes forward when the body moves forward. It can also go backward. It is powered <u>by batteries</u>. It is good for the environment because <u>it doesn't use gas</u>. The public was told about the invention on <u>December 3, 2001</u>.

The HT became available for purchase on
6 _____ (when). You have to
7 _____ (what) before you can drive it. You can carry packages on it, but not passengers. It travels
8 _____ (how fast). It doesn't have brakes because 9 _____ (why). It can be used
10 _____ (where). It can be driven on roads or even grass!

3   Work in small groups. What do you think are the advantages of the HT? What are the disadvantages?

Detective file: Student A

(For **B**'s part of this activity, go to page 111.)

1   Work with a partner. You both have some information about a missing person. Ask each other questions about the information you don't have to complete the chart.

2   With your partner, summarize the information about the person. Then talk about what you think has happened to this person and why the person is missing.

3   Compare your ideas with your class. Who had the most unusual idea?

Missing Person Report	
male or female:	
height:	
weight:	
hair color:	
eye color:	
occupation:	
when last seen:	Sunday morning
where last seen:	airport
destination:	Paris
wearing:	gray suit, dark blue coat, dark glasses
bank account status:	no money missing
objects missing from office:	small, very valuable painting; photograph of family

UNIT
9 **Detective file: Student B**

(For A's part of this activity, go to page 110.)

1 Work with a partner. You both have some information about a missing person. Ask each other questions about the information you don't have to complete the chart.

2 With your partner, summarize the information about the person. Then talk about what you think has happened to this person and why the person is missing.

3 Compare your ideas with your class. Who had the most unusual idea?

Missing Person Report	
male or female:	male
height:	six feet tall
weight:	125 pounds
hair color:	brown
eye color:	green
occupation:	bank manager
when last seen:	
where last seen:	
destination:	
wearing:	
bank account status:	
objects missing from office:	

UNIT
10 **What's right? What's polite?**

1 Work in small groups. Choose one of the people to role-play. Then pick a topic to discuss. Give your character's opinions about good and bad manners for the topic.

> greetings
> body language / personal space
> table manners
> dealing with salespeople or waiters
> visiting people's houses
> using cell phones
> smoking

Milly:	woman, 25, accountant, lives in a small town
Josh:	man, 32, chef, lives in a big city
Carlos:	man, 73, retired teacher, lives in a small town
Penelope:	woman, 47, actress, lives in a big city
Marvin:	man,18, student, lives in a small town
Tricia:	woman, 84, retired lawyer, lives in a big city

2 Pick different characters and discuss another topic.

3 Discuss what factors you think most affect people's opinions about manners.

> occupation   age   location   your ideas

UNIT 11 ▸ Game of Regrets

1   Work with a partner. Choose one of the situations. What might each person regret? What could have been done differently? Then choose another situation.

Example
Situation: Jaime won a million dollars and wasted all of the money.
He regrets that he wasted the money. If he hadn't wasted the money, he could have been wealthy now.

> SITUATIONS:
> • Jaime won a million dollars and wasted all of the money.
> • Elsa opened a small business, but it failed.
> • Your friend accepted the wrong job and is now very unhappy.
> • You bought a car that is too small and very unreliable.
> • Your neighbor's house was broken into and robbed.
> • Tammy and Sal went on vacation in Hawaii and had a terrible time.

2   Work with another pair. Compare your answers.

UNIT 12 ▸ Caption the Cartoons

1   Work in small groups. Look at cartoon A. Which caption do you think is the best?

What time would you like that wake up call?
Good morning, Officer Brown. I'll let him know you're calling…
It's been a slow day, so I'm just practicing.
Would you like to hear some music while you hold?

2   As a group, write your own captions for cartoons B and C.

3   Compare captions as a class. Which are the funniest? The most ridiculous?

A

"Would you like to hear some music while you hold?"

B

"No, I don't have an appointment.
I'm a birthday surprise."

C

"I'm afraid your dental plan does not cover tusks."

Vocabulary Reference

This section brings together key words and expressions from each unit. Use *Word for Word* to note down other important words that you want to remember.

Unit 1: From me to you

alpine (*adj.*)
ankle (*n.*)
auditory (*adj.*)
bark (*v.*)
beep (*v.*)
carved (*adj.*)
cheer (*v.*)
civilization (*n.*)
clap (*v.*)
code (*n.*)
collapse (*v.*)
complain (*v.*)
cyclone (*n.*)
drum (*n.*)
endurance (*n.*)
exhaustion (*n.*)
flu (*n.*)

footrace (*n.*)
frightened (*adj.*)
frontier (*n.*)
gossip (*n., v.*)
honk (*v.*)
horn (*n.*)
hum (*v.*)
jungle (*n.*)
marathon (*n.*)
messenger (*n.*)
ongoing (*adj.*)
pigeon (*n.*)
pony (*n.*)
post (*v.*)
reduce (*v.*)
remote (*adj.*)
scream (*v.*)

shout (*v.*)
signal (*n.*)
sociologist (*n.*)
tap (*v.*)
telegraph (*n.*)
tribe (*n.*)
victory (*n.*)
whisper (*v.*)
whistle (*v.*)

Expressions
Guess what!
keep in touch

Word for Word

Unit 2: In the limelight

accordion (*n.*)
album (*n.*)
audience (*n.*)
award-winning (*adj.*)
biography (*n.*)
bizarre (*adj.*)
blend (*v.*)
blues (*n.*)
calcium (*n.*)
claim (*v.*)
comet (*n.*)
competition (*n.*)
concerned (*adj.*)
crime (*n.*)
criticize (*v.*)
development (*n.*)

dissatisfied (*adj.*)
distraction (*n.*)
duration (*n.*)
emphasis (*n.*)
enormous (*adj.*)
fact (*n.*)
fast-paced (*adj.*)
folk (*adj.*)
fortune (*n.*)
funk (*n.*)
geography (*n.*)
hot-air balloon (*n.*)
hydrogen (*n.*)
influence (*n.*)
knowledge (*n.*)
literature (*n.*)

lyrics (*n.*)
measure (*v.*)
medical (*adj.*)
medieval (*adj.*)
melody (*n.*)
minimize (*v.*)
nitrogen (*n.*)
novel (*n.*)
opera (*n.*)
orchestra (*n.*)
oxygen (*n.*)
perpetual (*adj.*)
poem (*n.*)
process (*n.*)
professional (*adj.*)
reggae (*n.*)

regulate (*v.*)
rehearsal (*n.*)
require (*v.*)
revolution (*n.*)
rhythm (*n.*)
series (*n.*)
songwriter (*n.*)
sum (*n.*)
suspense (*n.*)
technical (*adj.*)
tongue (*n.*)
village (*n.*)
volcano (*n.*)

Unit 3: By coincidence

acquaintance (n.)
afterwards (adv.)
basis (n.)
bring up (v.)
chain (n.)
clinic (n.)
coincidence (n.)
come into (v.)
confirm (v.)
criteria (n.)
determined (adj.)
discovery (n.)
exhausted (adj.)
expectation (n.)
extensively (adv.)
fall for (v.)
following (adj.)
hypothesis (n.)
implication (n.)
interrupt (v.)
itinerary (n.)

location (n.)
melt (v.)
mysterious (adj.)
originally (adv.)
orphan (n.)
packet (n.)
pass away (v.)
pocket (n.)
previous (adj.)
randomly (adv.)
rapid (adj.)
reject (v.)
romance (n.)
run into (v.)
select (v.)
shelter (v.)
sleepless (adj.)
slip (v.)
stare (n.)
steal (v.)
target (n.)

theorize (v.)
tractor (n.)
tragic (adj.)
turn down (v.)
turn out (v.)
turn up (v.)
unexpectedly (adv.)
unfortunate (adj.)
wealthy (adj.)

Expressions
first-name basis
have the heart to
mixed up

Word for Word

Unit 4: A day's work

apply (v.)
brag (v.)
consultant (n.)
costume designer (n.)
cowgirl (n.)
deadline (n.)
detective (n.)
doll (n.)
firm (n.)
freedom (n.)
generalize (v.)
goal (n.)
grateful (adj.)
hardship (n.)
hire (v.)
import-export (adj.)
inspiring (adj.)
insurance (n.)
invoice (n.)
laboratory (n.)
mail carrier (n.)

marketing (adj., n.)
pastry (n.)
patient (n.)
pay check (n.)
pile (n.)
pizza chef (n.)
presentation (n.)
production (n.)
programmer (n.)
regret (v.)
reporter (n.)
representative (n.)
robot (n.)
roofer (n.)
seaman (n.)
staff (n.)
stock trader (n.)
studio (n.)
systems analyst (n.)
technician (n.)
temp (n.)

temporary (adj.)
toilet (n.)
tollbooth worker (n.)
unpleasant (n.)

Expressions
decompression
  sickness
job candidate
year in, year out
sick of

Word for Word

Unit 5: The nature of things

applaud (v.)
blizzard (n.)
boiling (adj.)
canoe (n.)
coexist (v.)
controversy (n.)
debris (n.)
deforestation (n.)
descend (v.)
domesticate (v.)
drought (n.)
earthquake (n.)
endanger (v.)
entrance (n.)
eruption (n.)
explode (v.)
export (n.)
fissure (n.)
flood (n.)
forecast (n.)
habitat (n.)

hunger (n.)
hurricane (n.)
hypothermia (n.)
inhabitant (n.)
insulation (n.)
knit (-ting) (v.)
lava (n.)
life jacket (n.)
mainland (n.)
mayor (n.)
mislead (v.)
oil-soaked (adj.)
opposition (n.)
overfishing (n.)
penguin (n.)
polarize (v.)
prevent (v.)
proportion (n.)
proposal (n.)
propose (v.)
pump (n.)

reintroduce (v.)
relocate (v.)
rescue (n.)
rescuer (n.)
resident (n.)
sheltered (adj.)
siren (n.)
spill (n.)
spray (n., v.)
starvation (n.)
steppes (n.)
sunscreen (n.)
thunderstorm
 (n.)
tornado (n.)
unpaved (adj.)
upside-down (adv.)
waterproof (adj.)

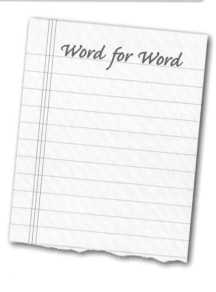

Word for Word

Expressions
catch fire
go canoeing

Unit 6: Make your mark

autograph (n.)
castle (n.)
character (n.)
cheat (v.)
detail (n.)
detective (n.)
disadvantaged (adj.)
disapproval (n.)
elegant (adj.)
emphasize (v.)
famous (adj.)
feminine (adj.)
folk tale (n.)
foolishness (n.)
greedy (adj.)
guilty (adj.)
hero (n.)
heroine (n.)
humorous (adj.)
independent (-ence)
 (adj., n.)

insist (v.)
kindness (n.)
lad (n.)
lesson (n.)
lie (v.)
majority (n.)
maturity (n.)
mild (adj.)
million-dollar (adj.)
moral (n.)
noodlehead (n.)
power (n.)
powerless (adj.)
quarter-finals (n.)
rarely (adv.)
recur (v.)
rescue (v.)
right (n.)
selfish (adj.)
sew (v.)
spark (n.)

stare (v.)
stepdaughter (n.)
succeed (v.)
tailor (n.)
trickster (n.)
trust (v.)
unimportant (adj.)
unwilling (adj.)
wave (v.)
windsurfer (n.)

Expressions
happy ending
learn a lesson
the letter of the
 law

Word for Word

Unit 7: By design

arch (n.)
attach (v.)
attempt (n.)
brake (n.)
bumper (n.)
canal (n.)
capture (v.)
challenge (n.)
chase (v.)
compact (adj.)
concrete (n.)
construct (-ion) (v., n.)
crack (n.)
cruise (v.)
dam (n.)
dashboard (n.)
destination (n.)
dig (v.)
dome (n.)
embankment (n.)
engine (n.)

fountain (n.)
gas mileage (n.)
gear shift (n.)
generate (v.)
ground (n.)
headlight (n.)
hood (n.)
irrigate (v.)
landmark (n.)
limousine (n.)
maintain (v.)
monument (n.)
oasis (n.)
passenger seat (n.)
pedestrian (n.)
prefabricated (adj.)
rely (v.)
reliable (-ility) (adj., n.)
resist (v.)
roadway (n.)
seat belt (n.)

span (v.)
statue (n.)
steering wheel (n.)
sunroof (n.)
suspend (v.)
suspension (adj.)
telescope (n.)
tower (n.)
transfer (v.)
tremendous
    (adj.)
trunk (n.)
tunnel (n.)
wagon (n.)
walkway (n.)
windshield (n.)

Word for Word

Expressions
a fan of
depending on
wild-goose chase

Unit 8: Special offer

awning (n.)
car service (n.)
chip (n., v.)
client (n.)
collapsible (adj.)
come off (v.)
commercial (n.)
commuter (n.)
complaint (n.)
confide (v.)
conventional (adj.)
convert (v.)
cozy (adj.)
cracked (adj.)
curve (n.)
damaged (adj.)
display (n.)
encounter (v.)
exchange (n.)
executive (n.)
fast food (n.)

faucet (n.)
fee (n.)
fitness (n.)
flier (n.)
flip (v.)
forbid (v.)
homemade (adj.)
house sitting (n.)
irritated (adj.)
leak (n., v.)
manned (adj.)
mattress (n.)
motion (adj.)
nuisance (n.)
official (n.)
permit (n.)
pharmacy (n.)
placement (n.)
post (v.)
pressure (n.)
ridiculous (adj.)

sandwich board
    (n.)
scratch (n.)
scratched (adj.)
sophisticated
    (adj.)
stain (n.)
technique (n.)
upscale (adj.)
utensil (n.)
window cleaner
    (n.)

Word for Word

Expressions
bad taste
drive someone
    crazy
fed up with
make someone mad

Unit 9: Mysteries and science

abandoned (*adj.*)
age-old (*adj.*)
bone (*n.*)
canyon (*n.*)
century (*n.*)
chain letter (*n.*)
chest (*n.*)
combination (*n.*)
contagious (*adj.*)
contract (*v.*)
creature (*n.*)
crocodile (*n.*)
cube (*n.*)
curved (*adj.*)
depressing (*adj.*)
dinosaur (*n.*)
disappear (*v.*)
disease (*n.*)
dozen (*n.*)
equator (*n.*)
excavate (*v.*)

factor (*n.*)
flourishing (*adj.*)
fossil (*n.*)
furious (*adj.*)
gasoline (*n.*)
glide (*v.*)
gorilla (*n.*)
intense (*adj.*)
jaw (*n.*)
lakebed (*n.*)
legend (*n.*)
length (*n.*)
long-dead (*adj.*)
mammal (*n.*)
meteor (*n.*)
mud (*n.*)
mystery (-ious)
   (*n., adj.*)
paleontologist (*n.*)
paleontology (-ist) (*n.*)
passionate (*adj.*)

pole (*n.*)
prehistoric (*adj.*)
relative (*n.*)
remains (*n.*)
sand (*n.*)
satisfactory (*adj.*)
settlement (*n.*)
shallow (*adj.*)
sheet (*n.*)
slippery (*adj.*)
star (*n.*)
steep (*adj.*)
stick (*n.*)
stone (*adj., n.*)
teeth (*n.*)
terrified (*adj.*)
torch (*n.*)
track (*n.*)
uncover (*v.*)
unravel (*v.*)

wander (*v.*)
witness (*n.*)

Unit 10: Mind your manners

block (*n., v.*)
chew (*v.*)
clarify (*v.*)
confident (*adj.*)
constant (*adj.*)
constructive (*adj.*)
desperate (*adj.*)
dissolve (*adj.*)
distinguish (*v.*)
double-parking (*n.*)
fault (*n.*)
futility (*n.*)
guideline (*n.*)
haiku (*n.*)
jealous (*adj.*)
lamppost (*n.*)
lean (*v.*)
model (*n.*)
nonviolent (*adj.*)
officer (*n.*)

politician (*n.*)
proud (*adj.*)
publicity (*n.*)
relieved (*adj.*)
risk taker (*n.*)
sedan (*n.*)
self-conscious (*adj.*)
sheer (*adj.*)
snap (*v.*)
soap opera (*n.*)
stack up (*v.*)
sticky (*adj.*)
stroller (*n.*)
threaten (*v.*)
toot (*n., v.*)
traffic jam (*n.*)
tree-lined (*adj.*)
vast (*adj.*)
vegetarian (*n.*)
violation (*n.*)

Expressions
honk the horn
make someone snap
push someone
   over the edge

Unit 11: Make or break

advise (v.)
alert (adj.)
armed (adj.)
arrest (v.)
banister (n.)
bench (n.)
blackmail (n.)
cartoonist (n.)
charge (v.)
chief (n.)
coach (n.)
comic strip (n.)
convict (v.)
court case (n.)
crash (v.)
drop by (v.)
drop out (v.)
excavator (n.)
fare (n.)
figure out (v.)
give up (v.)

graffiti (n.)
gratitude (n.)
hack (v.)
hang out (v.)
helmet (n.)
hypothetical (adj.)
jail (n.)
jewel (n.)
judge (n.)
jury (n.)
keep on (v.)
landlord (n.)
let down (v.)
mask (n.)
millennium (n.)
mug (-ging) (v., n.)
plain-clothes (adj.)
plead (v.)
priceless (adj.)
prison (n.)
punishment (n.)

put together (v.)
put up (v.)
raid (n.)
robber (n.)
robbery (n.)
shoplifting (n.)
snatch (v.)
spot (v.)
stroll (v.)
suggest (v.)
support (v.)
surround (v.)
suspect (v.)
take care of (v.)
trial (n.)
turn out (v.)
vandalism (n.)

Expressions
be into something
get on the wrong track
keep an eye on
scare the wits out of
under suspicion

Unit 12: A laugh a day

absent (adj.)
antibiotic (n.)
backstage (adj.)
benefit (n.)
brighten (v.)
come up with (v.)
caption (n.)
caricature (n.)
comedy (n.)
comical (adj.)
complement (v.)
connector (n.)
cream (n.)
cut down on (v.)
degrade (v.)
designated (adj.)
determined (adj.)
donate (v.)
examine (v.)
first-hand (adj.)
fever (n.)

get away with (v.)
get out of (v.)
grim (adj.)
healing (n.)
idiomatic (adj.)
incongruity (n.)
inspiration (n.)
interaction (n.)
joke (n.)
keep up with (v.)
laughter (n.)
lounge (n.)
make up for (v.)
management (n.)
measles (n.)
medication (n.)
occur (v.)
one-to-one (adj.)
operation (n.)
outcome (n.)
penicillin (n.)

prescription (n.)
proof (n.)
punch line (n.)
row (n.)
settle down (v.)
superior (-ity)
 (adj., n.)
surgeon (n.)
symptom (n.)
taboo (adj., n.)
tickle (v.)
treatment (n.)
vaccine (n.)
visual (adj.)
verbal (adj.)

Expressions
on call
quality of life

Grammar Reference

This section reviews and expands the main grammar points presented in this book.

Review of present and past forms		Unit 1
	Statements	**Questions**
Simple present Simple past	I live here. You don't live here. Tom lives here. Liz doesn't live here. I worked there. He didn't work there.	Do they live here? Does Jean live here? Did they work there?
Present continuous Past continuous	I'm (not) studying now. They are / aren't studying. I was / wasn't leaving. They were / weren't leaving.	Are you studying? Is she studying? Was she leaving? Were you leaving?
Present passive Past passive	That T-shirt is / isn't made of cotton. Oranges are / aren't grown in this area. It was / wasn't written in 1962. The houses were / weren't built in 1902.	Is the chair made of wood? Are the books sold here? Was it written in 1972? When were they built?

In the simple present, an -s or -(i)es is added to the end of the verb in the third person singular: *He / She reads, watches, studies.* In the simple past, the verb form is the same for all persons with both regular and irregular verbs.

The simple present and past use the auxiliaries *do, does,* and *did* to form negative statements and questions: *They do not read the newspaper on the weekends. He did not watch TV last night.*

Stative verbs are not usually used in the continuous: for example, *feel, hear, see, seem, think,* and *understand.*

Tag questions		Unit 1
	Statement	**Tag**
With be	You**'re** not working, It **was** a good movie,	**are** you? **wasn't** it?
With do / did	You **don't have** a car, Tom **got** a job,	**do** you? **didn't** he?
With have	You**'ve** seen this, It **hasn't** been raining,	**haven't** you? **has** it?
With modals	We **could** leave early, You **won't** say anything, Sally **can** drive, He **wouldn't** do that,	**couldn't** we? **will** you? **can't** she? **would** he?

Tag questions are used to confirm that something is true, to ask for agreement, or to make a request. Short answers are often used to respond to tag questions:
A: *It's a nice day, isn't it?* B: *Yes, it is.*

Answers to the *How Much Do You Know About Science?* quiz on page 75: 1a, 2c, 3a, 4b, 5c, 6c, 7b, 8b, 9a, 10b, 11a, 12b.

Present perfect continuous		Unit 2
Statements		
I/ You/ We/ They He/ She/ It	have / haven't been has / hasn't been	waiting for a long time.
Questions		*Answers*
Have you been waiting for a long time? How long have you been waiting?		Yes, I have. / No, I haven't. For an hour.
Present perfect simple		
Statements		
I/ You/ We/ They He/ She/ It	have / haven't has / hasn't	eaten all the food.
Questions		*Answers*
Have you eaten all the food? How much have you eaten?		Yes, I have. / No, I haven't. A lot.

The present perfect continuous is used for actions continuing up to the present, especially when there is an emphasis on how long the action has lasted. The present perfect continuous emphasizes the action in progress. In contrast, the present perfect simple emphasizes achievement or results. The present perfect continuous cannot be used with stative verbs like *know* or *believe*.

Questions with prepositions	Unit 2
What is Michael Crichton	famous **for**?
Michael Crichton	is famous **for his novels**.
Who did Magda	write **to**?
Magda	wrote **to her mother**.
Where does Simon	come **from**?
Simon	comes **from Britain**.

The most usual place for a preposition is at the end of a question.
In very formal speech or writing, the preposition sometimes comes before the question word, and *who* changes to *whom* after the preposition: *To whom are you writing?*

Past perfect			Unit 3
Statements			
Subject	**had**	**+**	*past participle*
I /You He /She We / They	had / hadn't		met the woman before.
Questions			*Answers*
Had you met the woman before? Where had you met her?			Yes, I had. / No, I hadn't. In Los Angeles.

The past perfect is used to show that something happened earlier than something else in the same sentence or context: *When we arrived at the theater, the movie had already started.*

Relative clauses		Unit 3
With relative pronoun as subject		
Paula is the woman	**that / who**	works in my office.
This is the letter	**that / which**	arrived this morning.
With relative pronoun as object		
Diana is the woman	**(that / who)**	I met at a party.
This is the letter	**(that /which)**	we were waiting for.
These are the books	**(that /which)**	I told you about.

When the relative pronoun is the object of the clause, it is often omitted: *Diana is the woman I met at a party. This is the letter we were waiting for.*

In very formal speech or writing, the preposition sometimes comes before the relative pronoun, and *who* is changed to *whom*: *Doris is someone with whom I work.*

Verbs followed by gerunds or infinitives	Unit 4
Verb + gerund (verb + -ing)	
I **suggest calling** the restaurant before we leave.	
I **got used to living** in the country.	
Verb + infinitive (to + base form)	
We've **decided to eat** out tonight.	
You **promised to call** me, but you didn't.	
Verb + gerund OR infinitive	
I've **started working** in an office. OR I've **started to work** in an office.	

Common verbs followed by a gerund: *don't mind, can't stand, enjoy, keep, suggest, can't help, look forward to, be / get used to.*

Common verbs followed by an infinitive: *want, plan, need, would like, hope, decide, offer, refuse, seem, promise.*

Common verbs followed by a gerund or an infinitive: *like, love, hate, start, begin, continue, prefer.*

It... + infinitive		Unit 4
It's + adjective	**It's nice to meet** you.	
	It's important to finish the project on time.	
It's a good idea	**It's a good idea to dress** formally for an interview.	
It takes time	**It takes a long time to learn** a new skill.	
It costs money	**It costs money to take** a vacation.	

Other expressions with *it... + infinitive* are: *it's possible, it's unusual, it's interesting, it's better.*

Passive verb forms			Unit 5
Continuous	*Subject*	**be** +	**being +** *past participle*
Present	The habitat The animals	is / isn't are / aren't	being threatened by pollution.
Past	The beach The birds	was / wasn't were / weren't	being cleaned yesterday.
Perfect	*Subject*	**have / has / had**	**+ been +** *past participle*
Present	The area The trees	has /hasn't have / haven't	been discovered yet. been cut down.
Past	The forest The beaches	had / hadn't had / hadn't	been cut down. been discovered yet.

The passive is used when the emphasis is on the process or action not on the performer
of the action.
A phrase with *by* is used to refer to the performer of the action if necessary: *The penguins were being
threatened by hypothermia.*

Time clauses (future)	Unit 5
Main clause	*Time clause*
The doctor will call us	**when** he **has** the results.
We'll be back home	**by the time** you **get** this postcard.
You can leave	**as soon as** the bell **rings**.
Don't open the door	**until** we **switch** off the alarm.

Time clauses can begin or end a sentence. When they begin a sentence, they are followed by
a comma: *I'll call you as soon as I get home.* OR *As soon as I get home, I'll call you.*

Expressing ability: *could* and *be able to*		Unit 6
Past	The athlete **could /couldn't** run very fast. He **was / wasn't able to** win a medal last year.	
Present perfect	David **has/ hasn't been able to** work this week. We **have/ haven't been able to** take a vacation this year.	
Future *Other forms*	You **will / won't be able to** go to college next fall. He **would / wouldn't be able to** help you if you asked him. They **might / might not be able to** come to the party.	

Could cannot be used to refer to a single event in the past.
Couldn't can refer to a single event in the past: *I'm sorry I couldn't come to the party.*
Couldn't can also refer to general ability in the past: *When he was younger, he couldn't play the guitar
very well.*

First conditional (possible or likely situations)   Unit 6

Statements

If the group is successful,	they'll sell a lot of albums.
If it doesn't rain tomorrow,	we'll go on a picnic.

Questions

What will we do	if it rains?
What will the boss say	if you don't go to work tomorrow?

Second conditional (hypothetical or imaginary situations)

Statements

If I were famous,	I would (I'd) quit my job.
If I didn't have this job,	I'd move to a smaller town.

Questions

What would you do	if you lost your job?
Where would you live	if you had a lot of money?

In the first conditional, a future form is used in the main clause and a present form in the *if* clause.
In the second conditional, *would, could,* or *might* is used in the main clause and past form in the *if* clause.
The order of the clauses can be reversed: *We'll go on a picnic if it doesn't rain tomorrow.*
Were is often used after *I, he, she,* or *it* in the second conditional, especially in formal situations or in the expression *If I were you...*

Passive forms: Modals   Unit 7

Statements

Subject	Modal + be + past participle
Some new laws	will be introduced this year.
Air pollution	must be reduced in this area.
Something	ought to be done about that.
Your car	has to be checked every two years.

Questions

Modal	Subject	be +	past participle
Should	anything	be	done to solve this problem?
How can	the situation	be	improved?

So / such (a)... + result clause   Unit 7

Main clause	Result clause
The movie was **so boring**	that I fell asleep.
The building cost **so much money**	that they couldn't afford to finish it.
We had **so many suitcases**	that we had to rent a van.
The camera was **such a bargain**	that everyone wanted one.
The document is written in **such difficult language**	that no one can understand it.

So is used before an adjective or a phrase with *much* or *many*. *Such (a)* is used before a noun or before a noun phrase: *It's such a disaster! He's such a good doctor. They're such great books!*

Have / get + object + past participle	Unit 8
Let's have We can get They had He got You've had She's gotten	these clothes cleaned. the house painted. copies made.

To *have* or *get something done* means to arrange for somebody else to do something.

Verb + object + infinitive (with *to*)	Unit 8
They	**got some friends to help** them.
My friends	**persuaded me to go** camping with them.
We	**expected it to rain,** but it didn't.

Verb + object + infinitive (without *to*)	
I'll	**let you borrow** my car if you do me a favor.
We	**had someone drive** us to the airport.

Verbs followed by an object + infinitive with *to*: *advise, allow, ask, expect, encourage, forbid, force, get, invite, need, order, persuade, remind, tell, want, warn.*
Verbs followed by an object + infinitive without *to*: *make, let, have.*
The word *help* can take either form: *I'll help you to choose.* OR *I'll help you choose.*

Past modals: Possibility (speculation)			Unit 9
Statements			
Where's Joan?			
I don't know.	She	may have might have could have	gone to the supermarket.
Her car's still here.	She	couldn't have	gone to the supermarket.
The dog's not here.	She	must have	taken the dog for a walk.

Question	Answer
This looks like Ben's jacket. **Could he have** left it here?	Yes, he **could have.**

May have, might have, and *could have* are used to describe possibility in the past (when you are not sure what happened). The negative forms are *may not have* and *might not have* (the full forms).
Couldn't have is used to describe something that was probably impossible (you are almost sure it did not happen).
Must have is used to describe strong probability or certainty in the past.

Noun clauses		Unit 9
With question words	I don't remember	**what I said.**
	We don't know	**why this happens.**
With whether / if	I wonder	**whether they're home yet.**
	She wants to find out	**if it's true.**
With that	Some people believe	**that they can foretell the future.**

Noun clauses often follow verbs like *know, explain,* or *understand.*
Noun clauses begin with a question word (*how, where, when*) or with *whether, if,* or *that.*
Whether and *if* have the same meaning, but *whether* is sometimes used in more formal situations.

Direct speech		Reported speech	Unit 10
Statements			
"It's on the second floor."		it **was** on the second floor.	
"I don't know."		he **didn't** know.	
"I can't help you."		he **couldn't** help me.	
"I'm going to work."	He said that	he **was going** to work.	
"I'll call you tomorrow."		he **would** call me tomorrow.	
"I haven't heard anything."		he **hadn't** heard anything.	
"I saw that movie."		he **had seen** that movie.	
Questions			
"Where is the office?"	She asked (them)	where **the office was.**	
"Did you enjoy the movie?"		whether **they had enjoyed** the movie.	

When reporting speech with a past tense verb (*he said, I told her, they explained*), the tense in the original sentence often moves back one degree: for example, present tenses become past, past tenses become past perfect, and *will* becomes *would.*

Past modals: *would have, should have* + past participle		Unit 10
Statements		
I should have called them earlier.	I would have apologized.	
I shouldn't have disturbed them.	I wouldn't have been so rude.	
Questions		
What should I have done?	What would you have done in my situation?	
Should I have said something?	Would you have done something different?	

The expressions *should have* and *would have* + past participle are used to hypothesize about events in the past. We often use *should have* and *would have* to describe what might have been a better course of action.

Third conditional (past unreal conditions)	Unit 11
If *clause (past perfect)*	**Main clause (past modal)**
If I hadn't been sick,	I would have gone to the party.
If you had told me it was your birthday,	we could have had a party.
If we hadn't had such a good coach,	we might never have won the competition.
Questions	
What would we have done	if you hadn't helped us?
If Gene hadn't played,	would you have won the game?

The third conditional is used to describe hypothetical or unreal situations in the past.
The order of the clauses can be reversed: *I would have gone to the party if I hadn't been sick.*

Clauses with *whatever, wherever, whoever, whenever*	Unit 11
We take the dog with us	**wherever we go.**
On vacation, you can do	**whatever you like.**
I'll call you	**whenever I get a chance.**
I don't want to talk to them,	**whoever they are.**
Whatever you do,	don't tell them my name.

Whatever, wherever, whoever, and *whenever* mean: *anything/ place/ person/ time* or *it doesn't matter what thing / place / person / time.*
When the main verb is in the future, the *-ever* clause is in the present.

Structures with *there + be*		Unit 12
	be	**Subject**
There	is going to be	a new library here soon.
	are going to be	a lot more people in the area.
	has been	an increase in unemployment this year.
	have been	several burglaries in the neighborhood.
	should be	a law against that kind of behavior.
	used to be	a movie theater here, but it closed.

There can be used with all forms of *be* (*is going to be, has been, will be, used to be,* etc.)
The verb form must agree with the subject of the sentence.

Connectors	Unit 12
Addition	also, in addition, besides
Contrast	however, nevertheless, on the other hand
Example	for example
Result	as a result, therefore, thus
Reason	because of this, for this reason
Similarity	similarly, in the same way
Sequence	first, second, next, then, finally

These connectors are used to make logical connections between sentences. They usually begin a sentence.
Frieda is an accomplished pianist. In addition, she plays the violin and the guitar.

Irregular Verbs

Base form	Simple past	Past participle	Base form	Simple past	Past participle
be	was/were	been	make	made	made
beat	beat	beaten	meet	met	met
become	became	become	pay	paid	paid
bend	bent	bent	put	put	put
break	broke	broken	quit	quit	quit
bring	brought	brought	read	read	read
buy	bought	bought	ride	rode	ridden
cast	cast	cast	ring	rang	rung
choose	chose	chosen	rise	rose	risen
come	came	come	run	ran	run
cut	cut	cut	say	said	said
dig	dug	dug	see	saw	seen
do	did	done	sell	sold	sold
draw	drew	drawn	send	sent	sent
drink	drank	drunk	set	set	set
drive	drove	driven	sew	sewed	sewn
eat	ate	eaten	shoot	shot	shot
fall	fell	fallen	show	showed	shown (showed)
fight	fought	fought	sing	sang	sung
find	found	found	sit	sat	sat
fit	fit	fit	sleep	slept	slept
fly	flew	flown	speak	spoke	spoken
forbid	forbid (forbade)	forbidden	spend	spent	spent
get	got	gotten (got)	stand	stood	stood
give	gave	given	steal	stole	stolen
go	went	gone	sweep	swept	swept
hang	hung	hung	swim	swam	swum
have	had	had	take	took	taken
hide	hid	hidden	teach	taught	taught
hold	held	held	tear	tore	torn
hurt	hurt	hurt	tell	told	told
keep	kept	kept	think	thought	thought
knit	knit	knit	throw	threw	thrown
know	knew	known	understand	understood	understood
lay	laid	laid	unwind	unwound	unwound
lead	led	led	upset	upset	upset
leave	left	left	wake	woke	waken
lend	lent	lent	wear	wore	worn
let	let	let	win	won	won
lose	lost	lost	write	wrote	written

Audioscripts

This section provides audioscripts where a reference and extra support for recorded activities may be helpful.

Unit 1

7b-c

I = Interviewer, C = Dr. Cohen

I: And today my guest is Dr. Andrea Cohen, a sociologist who is researching gossip. She knows all about how, why, and when we gossip. Gossip has a bit of a bad reputation, doesn't it?

C: Yes, indeed it does. We have an idea that gossip is—you know—people whispering about other people, saying bad things about people. That's a part of gossip, yes, but it's a very small part. Most gossip is perfectly harmless—and very natural.

I: Could you give us a definition of gossip?

C: Well, some sociologists define gossip as "informal talk about personal relationships."

I: About other people's personal relationships?

C: No, no, not necessarily. A lot of gossip is about our own relationships. We talk about our new boss, the problems we're having with our families, our colleagues, and our neighbors.

I: Well, by that definition I guess we all gossip a lot.

C: Absolutely. About two thirds of our informal conversation time is spent on these kinds of topics—social topics.

I: Interesting… . And now, do men gossip? It often seems to be more associated with women, but I think men do it, too.

C: Oh, yes. Actually, in terms of time spent on gossip, men gossip almost as much as women. But they spend more time talking about themselves!

I: Really?

C: Yes. Women talk about other people more.

I: Why do we gossip?

C: Well, that's really an interesting question. Basically gossip makes us feel like we're part of a community. And if you think about it, it's harder and harder to feel part of a community these days. Our families and friends often live quite a long way away these days. We may not even know our neighbors very well. So gossip helps us make connections with our community of friends and family.

I: So, does most gossip take place over the phone?

C: On the phone, yes, and now we have even more ways of gossiping by phone than we used to. People use their cell phones to have conversations while they're waiting for the bus. Teenagers are talking to their friends all the time, with text messaging for example. Technology is helping us stay in touch nowadays.

I: And to gossip more! Thank you, Dr. Cohen…

12b-c, 13a

T = Terry, V = Vince

V: Hi, Terry. It's Vince.

T: Hi, Vince. How are you doing?

V: Pretty good. How are you?

T: OK.

V: You don't sound good, Terry.

T: Well…I have a cold.

V: You should take a day off.

T: I can't because I have a meeting at work tomorrow. Did you hear about Abby?

V: No. What?

T: She broke her ankle. She fell on her way to work.

V: Oh, my goodness! Is she OK?

T: She's OK but she can't run in the marathon next week, so she's pretty mad about that.

V: Oh, that's too bad. She's been training for months, hasn't she?

T: Yes. She runs a lot. I could never run in a marathon.

V: Me neither. By the way, how's Josh doing?

T: Well…he finally got a job.

V: That's good news. Where?

T: At a software company. He had an interview and they liked him, so he starts next week.

V: That's great.

T: Yes. It's a good company.

V: Where's the company?

T: Oh…not too far away. About twenty minutes from here.

V: So he's going to drive?

T: No. He'll probably take the bus. There's a direct bus from our place to the office. So he's going to try that first.

V: That sounds good.

T: Yes, I think so. Anyway, I have to go. I'm in the middle of cooking dinner.

V: Oh, before I forget…I'm having a dinner party for Elaine. It's her birthday. Can you and Josh come?

T: Yes, I think so. I'll ask him tonight when he gets in.

V: OK. Great.

T: Hang on a minute… .When's the party?

V: Oh, yes, sorry! It's on Sunday…about 7:00.

Unit 2

1b-c

E = Erin, I = Interviewer

I: Welcome, Erin. Now…you sing with the San Francisco Opera, don't you?

E: Yes, I do.

I: How long have you been singing professionally?

E: About seven years.

I: Really? Tell me about it. What do you do exactly?

E: Well, I'm in the chorus, which means I sing with other people and perform in several operas in one season. Sometimes I have a real role—a bigger part with solos.

I: What roles have you played?

E: Last year I was Suzuki in *Madame Butterfly*. This year I'm Hansel in *Hansel and Gretel*. I've had several boys' roles, actually.

I: Oh? Why is that?

E: I guess it's because of the way I look. You know, I'm thin and not very tall.

I: Well, you certainly don't look like a typical opera singer.

E: No, I know.

I: So…how did you get into this?

E: Well, I always loved to sing, and I sang as a hobby for a long time. Then I realized I needed some lessons, so I got a voice teacher. She suggested that I try out for the opera. So I did. And they wanted me. I couldn't believe it! I never thought I'd do this for a living.

I: That's wonderful. You've found your calling.

E: Yes, I really have. I've been incredibly lucky.

I: Do you get nervous before you go on stage?

E: Oh, yes. The first time I went on stage, I was so nervous I almost couldn't sing. I thought, "What am I doing here? I don't belong here, they've made a mistake!" For a long time, I wasn't very confident. Now I'm much more relaxed on stage. But I still get nervous, especially if I have a role.

I: What are you working on now?

E: For the last few months we've been working on *The Magic Flute*. But we've done that one before, so it's not too hard. We're also working on three others for the fall.

I: Wow! That's a lot! What's your schedule like?

E: Hectic! It's very hard work. When the opera is in season, I'm in performances until midnight, six days a week. In addition, we have hours of rehearsals, every day. And I have to practice at home.

I: Do you have time for anything else?

E: Well, it's hard to have a social life because I work in the evenings. That's one of the problems. But let's see… I love to go rock climbing. I do that about ten hours a week and on weekends. Oh, and I've been learning to play the accordion. I haven't learned very much yet, so I play badly. Very badly! But when I come home in the evenings I play it anyway, and it helps me to wind down.

6a-b

J = Janice, L = Larry, M = Mario, Re = Rena, Ru = Rudy

L: OK, let's have some music. Can anybody sing a song?

Ru: Not me. I can't sing.

J: Mario can. Mario, why don't you sing a song?

M: Oh, no. Honestly I'm not…

L: Oh, come on, Mario!

M: I'd really rather not.

J: OK. Rena, what about you? Can you sing something?

Ru: Yes! Come on, Rena! You can do it!

Re: Well, OK, as long as you all join in.

10b

P = Presenter, B = Barbara

P: Ladies and gentlemen, welcome to "What's the answer?" Our first contestant tonight, coming from Madison, Wisconsin, is Barbara Holbrook. Welcome to the show, Barbara.

B: Thank you.

P: It says here you're a librarian. Is that correct?

B: Yes. I work for the Public Library.

P: Do you read a lot?

B: Quite a lot, yes.

P: What are your favorite subjects?

B: I read a lot of biographies. I like science fiction, too.

P: And your husband's name is David. Is he here with you?

B: Yes, he's here.

P: Where is he? Is David in the audience? Oh, there he is. All right, let's have a hand for Barbara and David!

10c-d

P = Presenter, B = Barbara

P: All right, Barbara. First question, are you ready?

B: Yes, I guess.

P: For one hundred dollars. What country is risotto from? Is it A Spain, B Kenya, or C Italy?

B: Umm…Italy.

P: C, Italy is correct! Now, question number two. What does water consist of? Is it…A Hydrogen and oxygen, B Hydrogen and calcium, or C Oxygen and nitrogen?

B: H_2O…A. Hydrogen and oxygen.

P: A is correct! Water consists of hydrogen and oxygen. You're doing well so far, Barbara. How are you on sports?

B: Average, I guess.

P: Average. Well let's see if you can get this one. In boxing, what do the letters K.O. stand for? Is it A keep on, B kick over, or C knock out ?

B: That's C. Knock out.

P: C is correct! All right Barbara, you have one more question to finish the round with one thousand dollars. Are you ready?

B: Yes, I am!

P: What is a seismograph used for? Is it used for… A observing planets, B measuring land movements, or C regulating temperature?

B: Umm…It's not used for observing planets. It's not regulating temperature. I think it's…measuring land movements. B.

P: The answer is indeed B! Congratulations! You have won a thousand dollars!

11c

W = Woman, M = Man

W: Number 1. Who was Princess Diana married to?

M: Prince Charles.

W: Number 2. What is cheese made from?

M: Milk.

W: Number 3. What do the letters VCR stand for?

M: Video cassette recorder.

W: Number 4. Who was the Boy Scout movement founded by?

M: Robert Baden-Powell.

W: Number 5. What is the movie *Jurassic Park* about?

M: Dinosaurs.

W: Number 6. Where did the game of baseball originally come from?

M: England.

Unit 3

1b-c

In 1947, my mother, Deborah, was a twenty-one year old student at New York University, studying English literature. My father, Joseph was an art teacher. On Saturdays, he often painted all day and then went out for a meal. One Saturday, he chose a neighborhood restaurant called the Milky Way.

The Milky Way happened to be my mother's favorite restaurant, and that Saturday, she went there for dinner, carrying a used copy of Charles Dickens's *Great Expectations*. The restaurant was crowded, and she was given the last table. Reading her book, she quickly lost touch with what was going on around her. When the waitress came over and asked her if she would mind sharing her table with someone, she agreed without even looking up from her book.

"A tragic life for poor, dear Pip," my father said when he saw the tattered cover of *Great Expectations*. My mother looked up at him, and to this day she says she saw something familiar in his eyes.

Whatever it was that my parents saw, heard, or felt that night, they both understood that something unusual had happened. They talked for hours. Later, my mother wrote her telephone number on the inside of *Great Expectations* and gave the book to my father. He said goodbye, and they went off in opposite directions. That night, neither one of them was able to sleep.

6b-c

J = John, M = Man, W = Woman

J: An amazing thing happened to my father a few months ago. Listen to this. I have to tell you this story.

M: Let's hear it!

W: Yes! Of course!

J: OK. Well as you know my dad—Franco—is from Italy. He was born and raised in a small town in Sicily. And when he was 18 years old, he and his brother went to a town called Ramacca, to find work on a farm. Well, when they were working on the farm they met another two brothers, and they all became close friends. But one day, there was an accident and one of the other guys hit my father with a tractor.

W: Ouch! Was he hurt badly?

J: Yes, he was, actually. He had to go into the hospital for six months! Of course, the guy who was driving the tractor felt terrible about what happened. It was an accident, you know.

M: I'm sure.

J: But anyway...my dad went to the hospital, the brothers moved on, and they all lost touch. Eventually, my father came to America, married my mother, and now they live right here in New York.
Well...a few months ago my parents were at a wedding. My mother recognized a woman, Giuseppina, from the neighborhood. They started talking and the women introduced their husbands. They found out that they were all originally from Sicily. Giuseppina's husband said he once lived in Ramacca. My father said that he had lived there, too. The other guy said that he lived there 49 years ago, and worked on a farm.

M: No! I don't believe it!

W: Shhh... . Listen to the story!

J: Yes. You know where this is going, right? My father said, "That's funny, I worked on a farm then, too." So the other guy said, "Were you there with your brother?" and my father said yes. And at the same time they both realized who the other person was! My dad said, "You're Benedetto! You're the one that hit me with a tractor!" They jumped up and hugged each other and neither of them could believe it! Benedetto was so pleased to see that my father was OK, because he had never found out what happened to him after the accident.

M: That's amazing!

J: Yes. And even more amazing, it turned out that Benedetto has been living in the very same neighborhood as my parents for the past 28 years!

M: Wow! What a story!

W: That's incredible!

J: It is! And now they're close friends again.

11a-b

(CONVERSATION A)

A = Anne, L = Lindsey, M = Marco

A: Lindsey, I'd like you to meet Marco Freitas.

L: How do you do. Are you the politician that Anne told me about?

M: Well, I'm not really a politician. But I work in government, yes.

L: Well, I'm delighted to meet you. I've heard a lot about you.

(CONVERSATION B)

M = Man, S = Suki, W = Woman

W: This is Suki. She's from Kyoto, Japan.

M: Glad to meet you. Kyoto's the place where they have the beautiful gardens, isn't it?

S: Yes, that's right. Have you been there?

M: Not exactly in Kyoto. I was about ten miles from there.

(CONVERSATION C)

M1 = Man 1, M2 = Man 2

M1: Let me introduce you to Raisa. She's over there.

M2: Raisa? Is that the woman you were going out with last year?

M1: Oh no! That was Renee.

M2: Oh yes, that's right. I got the names mixed up.

Unit 4

1b-c

1 [Ryan: Pizza chef]

People keep asking me if I'm sick of pizza. And I say, "Sure, after making it and smelling it all day, of course I am." I eat pizza at work, but I refuse to eat it at home. If my family wants to order out, I say "That's fine, but I want Chinese food."

2 [Alex: Stock trader]

I've stopped telling people I work on Wall Street. People always start asking me questions about stocks: what should they invest in, what stocks are going up and down, and so on. Now I just say I work in accounting. Nobody wants to know about accounting.

3 [Nigel: Costume designer]

I work in the movies, so I sometimes get to meet movie stars and people who are famous. After a while you get used to working with them. They're just like everyone else. Of course everyone wants to know which ones are nice, and which ones are hard to work with. People always ask me, "What's he really like?" or "What's she really like?" What am I supposed to say? I usually just say they're very nice.

4 [Ed: Tollbooth worker]

People ask me why I decided to do this job. Most people think it's really boring. So they ask me about that. "How can you do this for 8 hours at a time?" Other typical questions are "How many breaks do you get?" and "What happens if you need to go to the bathroom?" I tell them, I don't mind working for 8 hours...we get breaks every couple of hours. Otherwise, we just have to wait.

5 [Melissa: Sales person]

"How much of a discount do you get?" I'm tired of hearing that question. It's like I took the job because I wanted the discount. It's kind of rude when you think about it. It's like asking someone how much money they make. OK, OK, I get a 30% discount!

5a

P = Paul, J = Justin

P: What does Stephanie do?

J: I'm not sure exactly. She has something to do with computers.

P: Does she work in sales?

J: No, I think she's a kind of consultant. She goes to companies, sets up their computer systems, and that kind of thing.

P: Oh, I see. She's a systems analyst.

J: Well, something like that, anyway.

8b

Good morning, and welcome to our show. Have you ever wanted to be a cowboy, out riding the range? Or a seaman, on the high seas in search of adventure? Well, you may want to think again. In a recently published report by *New View* magazine, the exciting occupations of cowboy and seaman were ranked least desirable—that is, in the bottom ten out of 250 occupations. Why is this? Well, they may be exciting, but they're also hard work, low-paying, physically dangerous, and stressful. Other unpopular jobs are: dancer, taxi driver, fisherman, construction worker, and roofer. But wait a minute. Aren't there still people who like these jobs? We wanted to find out, so we talked to some people who know.

8c-d

I = Interviewer, M = Michael, C = Connie, P = Phil

I: Here is Michael Lowrimore, who has a roofing company in Seattle, Washington.

M: Mostly, I like being outdoors in the spring and summer, not in a four-walled office all day. I can hear the birds, and I can watch the sun travel across the sky. Plus, I enjoy working in different places around town. I might be in one house for three days, then go to a new neighborhood and meet new people.

I: Phil Toth is retired now after spending 30 years on the high seas, as a seaman in the navy.

P: If you're a seaman and enjoy your job, you must be crazy. Well, I am crazy, and I did enjoy it. The pay was low, and the work was dangerous. But I don't regret doing it for a moment. I learned to be a leader, and I liked the action and excitement. When the weather gets rough, you don't have time to think. You just do it. Would I do it again? Yes! I always loved the job.

I: Here is Connie Kelts, whose family runs the Bar JJ Ranch in Alberta, Canada.

C: I don't know why they rated cowboy so low. I can't imagine doing anything else. It's a great job. Sure we work long days, but you get a lot of satisfaction from doing a hard day's work. Since the work is seasonal, you get a lot of free time. If you want to go fishing, you just go. No one tells you what to do. So, I won't ever get rich, but I wouldn't change my lifestyle for the world.

I: So for some people at least, the worst jobs aren't so bad after all.

Unit 5

4b-c

R = Ranger, V1 = Vistor 1, V2 = Visitor 2

R: Welcome to the park. Are you having a good time?

V1: Yes, but it's very crowded. So many people! It never used to be like this.

R: Yes. It gets very crowded in the summer now.

V1: Is that why the roads are closed?

R: Exactly. There was just too much traffic. You have to take a shuttle bus now, or walk or bike into the Valley.

V2: I guess people don't like that too much.

R: You know, people complain, but it's actually made the situation much better. The air is cleaner, and it's a lot quieter without all the traffic. The shuttle buses are electric. They don't pollute, and they're much quieter.

V2: Yes, it is quieter, now that you mention it.

R: And that's something we want to preserve in the national parks. There are so few places nowadays where you can go and hear only the sounds of nature.

V1: Hmmm…that's right. What about camping? Do you still allow camping?

R: Oh, yes! You can camp. But you have to make a reservation well in advance because the campgrounds are very popular.

V1: But I suppose campers are hard on the environment, too.

R: Well, we can minimize that if people cooperate. And most campers are fairly careful about fires, and that kind of thing. But we have to make sure that people keep their food in locked containers. That's a bit harder.

V1: Why do they have to keep food locked?

R: Because of the bears.

V2: Oh, you mean they try to get your food?

R: Yes. Unfortunately, some bears have gotten used to our food and they've developed a taste for things like tuna fish sandwiches. They'll even eat toothpaste and shampoo. Anything that smells interesting.

V2: Oh, my goodness!

R: I know! We want the animals to return to their natural feeding habits. Our food isn't good for them. It can make them sick, and if they get too dependent on human food they can become a danger to people. Sometimes we have to shoot them, if they're a big problem.

V1: Really?

R: Yes. So feeding wild animals actually endangers them. We really emphasize to people not to leave food around.

6a-b

G = Guide, M = Mark, W = Wendy

G: Do you all have your life jackets?

M: We sure do!

G: OK. Don't forget to keep your life jackets on all the time. And take sunscreen with you, in case it gets sunny. Put your clothes in a plastic bag so that they don't get wet.

M: Oh, OK. Make sure you don't lose the car keys, Wendy!

W: I've got them right here. Which way should we go?

G: Go down that way. Watch out for the big rocks at the bend in the river. The water moves very fast down there. And be careful! Don't stand up in the boat!

M: We won't! Thanks!

G: Have a good trip!

9b-c

So, what was the weather like in the United States this past year? Well, it was a very typical year for weather. As usual, we had a little of everything.

Let's go back to the beginning of the year. Early in January, we saw record low temperatures around the Great Lakes, as cold air moved down from the north, and temperatures dropped throughout the northern plains. Severe blizzards brought more than 20 inches of snow to Michigan and Wisconsin in one week. Airports were closed throughout the area, and air traffic was brought to a standstill.

In March, a heat wave brought record high temperatures to the South and the Southwest. High temperatures caused wildfires in Texas that burned more than 100,000 acres of land. The drought continued through the summer.

In May, there were severe thunderstorms in the Mississippi Valley and tornadoes in several states. A record 42 twisters hit Illinois in one day! Several homes were destroyed.

In September, the Gulf Coast was pounded by hurricanes and tropical storms. Winds up to 145 miles per hour caused widespread damage. Torrential rain brought major floods to the area. In Florida, 5,000 people were evacuated from their homes and taken to emergency shelters.

So all in all, it was a typical year. Some good, some bad. Let's hope that this year…

Unit 6

1b-c

My hero is Wilma Rudolph. She was a great runner in the 50s. But when she was very young she had polio, and she couldn't walk. She had to wear braces on her legs, and the doctors said she would never be able to walk again. But she was so determined! She worked very hard, and she not only walked again, but she went on to win three gold medals in the Olympics. Pretty amazing!

When I was a kid I read all the Nancy Drew books. Nancy Drew was a teenage detective and she was really clever. She could solve any crime. She was independent, too: she drove around in her own sports car. She got into all kinds of tricky situations, but she always managed to get out of them. And of course, she always solved the mysteries in the end. I used to dream about being Nancy Drew, I think mainly because of the car!

I admire people who risk their lives to save people. We live on the coast and we have a fantastic volunteer coastguard. Whenever people on a boat, or wind surfers or whatever, get into trouble in the water, they go out and rescue them, no matter what the weather is like. I really admire them. They just say, hey, someone's got to do it.

I really admire my dad, Arturo Salinas. He's sixty years old now, but he brought up four kids on his own after my mom died. He worked full-time, but he somehow managed to feed us all and take care of us when we were sick. He made sure we were all on time for school, and we couldn't play until we did our homework. You couldn't argue with him about that. I didn't like it at the time, but he was a great influence on my life.

10b-c

C = Cora, L = Lewis, S = Sheena, P1 = Person 1,
P2 = Person 2, P3 = Person 3,

L: And finally tonight, we have statistical proof of Americans' eternal optimism. According to a recent Harris poll on the subject of fame, it seems that 30%— that's nearly one third—of all adults in the United States believe that they are somewhat likely to become famous for at least 15 minutes.

S: That's incredible, isn't it? How could all those people become famous? And what would they do if they did?

L: Well, the interviewers also asked people how they would use their fame, if they became famous. Many people said they would make their business better known, or they would use their fame to get a better job. But a majority said they would also help people who are less fortunate than themselves.

S: Oh, that's nice.

L: Yes. It seems like we're a generous bunch.

S: In theory, at least!

L: Yes. Let's go now to Cora Segal, who's on the street with a live report. Cora?

C: Well, Lewis, I'm here in downtown, and I'm trying to find out how many people believe they're going to be famous. So far I haven't found very many! Excuse me… ma'am? I'm from WCBX TV and I'd like to ask you a question. Do you believe that you'll be famous in your lifetime?

P1: Oh my goodness, I hope not! I'd hate it! So I think it's very unlikely.

C: What would you do if you were famous?

P1: Oh! I don't know. I'd hate it. I wouldn't give any interviews, anyway.

C: Excuse me…sir? Could I ask you a question?

P2: Sure.

C: Do you think that you'll be famous in your lifetime?

P2: Who me? No, not a chance. Well I guess I might win the lottery or something. But the chances of that happening are pretty small!

C: If you were famous, how would you use your fame?

P2: Use it? Oh, wow. I don't know. Umm…I guess it would be nice to help other people somehow. But it would be hard to do unless I had a lot of money, too.

C: Thank you, sir. Hello… Miss… What are the chances that you'll be famous in your lifetime?

P3: I'd say it's pretty likely.

C: Really?

P3: Well, I hope so. I'm a musician. I've recorded a CD, and I'm appearing on TV next week. If that goes well, I might get a recording contract…and be a little famous.

C: So what will you do if you're successful?

P3: Well, if things go well, I'll quit my day job and play music full-time. That's what I really want to do.

C: Hmm…maybe I'd better get your autograph.

P3: Sure. You never know. You might be able to sell it.

12a

G = Gary, N = Nina, B = Beth

G: So what do you think? What are the chances that Naomi Lindberg will get the best actress award?

N: Not a chance. Not against Jessica Murray.

B: Oh, I don't know. I'd say it's likely. She gave a fantastic performance in that movie.

G: I agree. Jessica Murray got it last year. I bet they'll give it to Naomi Lindberg.

N: I guess they might. You never know!

Unit 7

3b-c

G = Guide, T1 = Tourist 1, T2 = Tourist 2

G: Right behind me is the Brooklyn Bridge. This is often called New York City's most beautiful bridge. It was completed in 1883 and it took fifteen years and cost 15 million dollars to build. When it was built, it was the world's longest suspension bridge. These two towers were just about the tallest structures in the city at that time.

T1: Who designed the bridge?

G: The bridge was designed by John Roebling, but he died after an accident early in the project. It was his son Washington Roebling who actually managed and completed the project. It was a huge project and quite dangerous.

T2: Why? Did people fall from the bridge?

G: Actually, the main danger was decompression sickness.

T2: Decompression sickness? What's that?

G: Decompression sickness is what happens when you come back up too quickly from being deep underwater. The two towers had to be sunk into the mud at the bottom of the river, so workers had to work down there. They were lowered into the water in large wooden boxes. Coming back up, they got air bubbles in their bloodstream. Several of the workers died or became ill from that.

T2: Wow!

G: Washington Roebling himself got sick in the middle of the project and he couldn't continue. He had to stay in bed, so he directed the rest of the project from his bedroom window, using a telescope. He dictated his orders to his wife, and she told the workers what to do.

Some people say she was really the one who built the bridge in the end.

T1: That's an incredible story. Was this the first bridge across the river?

G: It was the first bridge to go across the East River, so it was very important, and a lot of people used it. It cost a penny per person—one cent—to walk across the bridge, and ten cents to drive a one-horse wagon across. Five cents for a horse or a cow. So don't go bringing any horses or cows across the bridge now. It might get expensive!

9b-c

1: My first car was a 1960s Rambler. This was in the 1980s, so the car was twenty years old then. It was a big, blue and black thing. You changed gears by pushing a button! There were buttons on the dashboard that you pushed when you wanted to go into low gear. It was so heavy it got terrible gas mileage—about eight miles to the gallon. It didn't have much power so it was pretty slow. It felt like driving a boat. But I thought my car was wonderful. Now when I look at pictures of myself in it I realize I looked so tiny behind the steering wheel. You could hardly see me!

2: When I was a teenager I went to France and the family that I stayed with had a little Citroën. That was such a great car. I'm not really a car person but I loved that one. It was different from anything that I'd ever seen in the States. It was very economical. It got good mileage. But mainly I liked it because it was so European. It just had so much style. Citroëns were very fashionable at the time. All the young people in France drove them.

3: My friend Sharon had a 1970s pickup truck for years. It was such a beauty. It was about 25 years old, bright red, and in fantastic condition. She got it from the original owner and took really good care of it. It ran really well and it was very reliable. It never broke down. She didn't drive it every day and she didn't drive it at all in the winter, but we had a lot of fun going for rides in it. Everybody stopped and looked. Sometimes people would ask if it was for sale but she always said no. In fact, I think she still has it.

Unit 8

2b-c

I = Interviewer, V = Veronica

I: Your slogan is "You need it. We do it." Tell me about some of the things that people need and that you do.

V: We do the kinds of things that busy people don't have time to do. Things like buying and choosing gifts and getting them mailed, and just running errands like going to the post office, getting things cleaned, and so on.

I: Why did you decide to start this service?

V: Well, it came from my own experience. I was working full-time, and I just couldn't find the time to get anything done. I realized that there must be a lot of other people out there in the same situation. So I set up my own company. Now I run errands full-time!

I: And you can make a living doing that?

V: Yes, you can. I don't just do errands for people. I help them in their homes as well.

I: Really? What kind of things do you do there?

V: Well a lot of people need help organizing their closets, for example. For some people, it's paperwork: bills and bank statements and so on. They just need help organizing it. Sometimes I help people move. One guy

needed to set up a kitchen in his new apartment. He had no idea where to put everything!

I: What's the most interesting thing that you've been asked to do?

V: Well, one lady asked me to organize a surprise party for her husband's birthday. She travels a lot for business, so she couldn't do it herself. So she gave me a list of people to invite, and told me the kind of things she wanted. I had to find a location, arrange food and entertainment and everything else. That wasn't particularly unusual, but it was a lot of fun. I really enjoyed it.

I: I suppose if it's not your party, in a way, it's easier to enjoy the preparations.

V: Yes, and of course you're being paid for it. That helps!

I: Do you advertise?

V: Not much. Most of my business comes from recommendations now. People tell their friends. Basically for a lot of people, time is really precious, and they don't want to waste it running errands. They have the attitude, why should I do it myself if I can have it done by somebody else?

6a-b

R = Rob, S = Sheila

R: Look at this! This was a brand new shirt. I sent it to the cleaners, and look. It's torn—right here—and there's a button missing. It's ridiculous!

S: That's pretty bad.

R: I can't believe it! This happens almost every time I take something to the cleaners. It really drives me crazy.

S: You should probably go back and complain.

R: Well, I will, but I don't know why they don't do it right the first time. I'm fed up with it. That's the last time I send anything there.

S: Wait a minute…

R: What?

S: That's an old shirt that you sent. It was already torn. The new shirt is right here…and it's fine, Rob.

R: Oh! Oh, good!

10b-c

This weekend, Mattress Matters in downtown Princeton is having our grand opening sale. This weekend only, we're selling single, double, queen, and king size mattresses. You'll find all the top brand names at fantastic discounts. Check out the huge grand opening sale at Mattress Matters in downtown Princeton, at 408 Pine Avenue. Hurry! The sale is this weekend only! Mattress Matters. For a good night's sleep.

We know you have a lot to do. That's why the pharmacy at Superprice is open six days a week from 9:00 a.m. until 6:00 p.m. Stop by the store, or call in your prescription any time, and drop by to pick it up. While you're in the store, check out the Superprice savings on fresh produce—peaches at 79 cents a pound, delicious ripe tomatoes at 89 cents a pound, and potatoes at just two dollars a bag. Stock up on pasta: this week at Superprice all pasta is on sale at 50 percent off. And before you leave, stop by our florists to pick up a beautiful bunch of flowers for Mother's Day. We know you're busy. Superprice helps you save time. We have it all in one location!

M = Man, A = Announcer, W = Woman

M: Happy birthday darling. I got this for you.

W: Oh! What is it?

M: It's a garage door opener. I thought you'd like it.

W: Yes…oh yes. Thank you!

A: Do you have trouble buying gifts for the people you

love? Are you looking for just the right thing for that special person? We can help. Log on to whattogive.khw and choose from an incredible selection of gifts at prices you can afford. We have special offers every month and free delivery for purchases over 50 dollars. So what are you waiting for? Log on to whattogive.khw, and find something she really likes.

M: Happy birthday darling. I got this for you.

W: A gold bracelet! Oh, this is beautiful! Oh, what a beautiful present! Oh, thank you!

A: Whattogive.khw. The online shopping service for you!

Unit 9
4b and 4d

This happened about twenty years ago, in Germany, when I was visiting a town in the south with some friends. It was kind of a depressing town, with a lot of old, gloomy buildings. I remember it was raining, too. It was miserable weather. We were having dinner in a hotel restaurant. It was big and dark, and it felt old, though it really wasn't. Anyway I needed to use the bathroom so I asked the waitress where it was. She gave me an enormous key and said, "It's through there. Go out into the hallway, down the stairs, and it's the first door on the left."

So I went off with this huge key, all the way to the back of the restaurant, and found myself in a gray stone hallway. The first door on the left was large and heavy. It didn't look like a bathroom door, but I thought, well this must be it… . So I pulled the door open—I didn't actually need the key—and it opened with this creaking noise. I found myself looking into complete darkness. It was completely black.

So, I thought I'd made a mistake and I turned around to go. And suddenly, out of the corner of my eye, I saw this big ugly hand reaching out at me from the darkness. It scared me to death. I was terrified. I just ran, all the way back through the restaurant to my friends at the table.

4c

So, I went back and I told my friends what had happened. I said to my friend Mary, "You'll have to come back there with me. I'm not going back there by myself." Mary thought I was crazy, but she went with me anyway, and she opened the door. I stayed way back. She looked behind the door. And she started to laugh. She said, "It's a rubber glove, Julie. It's a rubber glove on top of a broom handle." Someone had stuck a broom behind the door and put a glove on top of it. But…I'll tell you…it was very lifelike.

11b-c and 12a

A = Anchor, G = Goodwin, T = Torres

A: Welcome to the World of Science. Our first question from our viewers today is, "Is it possible to travel at the speed of light?" That's a big one. Let me pose the question to our space expert here, Dr. Susanna Goodwin.

G: The answer to that is probably no. And I don't think it will ever be possible.

A: I see.

G: You know, if you did travel at the speed of light, time would go more slowly.

A: What do you mean?

G: Well, say, for example, you went on a spaceship, traveling at the speed of light, to visit a star that was—let's say—ten light years away. On earth it would take more than 22 years for that to happen. But on the spaceship, time would go more slowly. It would only

take you ten years to go and come back. Do you see what I mean?

A: Wait a minute. Sorry, but I don't get it. It would take you ten years in space, but that would be 22 years on earth?

G: Exactly.

A: But what I don't understand is, would that ten years feel like ten years—or like 22 years?

G: To you on the spaceship, it would feel like ten years.

A: And when you got back, you'd be twelve years younger than everyone else?

G: That's right.

A: I see…amazing! Thank you, Dr. Goodwin. Well, let's move on to our next question. Why do people yawn? Let's give that one to Vic Torres.

T: Yes, I can answer that one. Yawning is actually a very interesting phenomenon, and nobody's really quite sure why we do it.

A: We yawn when we're tired, don't we?

T: Well, that's what most people think, but we're not sure about that. We now believe that yawning is social behavior. For one thing, it's very contagious. You know what I mean?

A: You mean, when you yawn, I yawn.

T: Yes. We're programmed to respond in that way. Well, some people believe that yawning was originally a way to synchronize group behavior—to make sure that everybody did the same thing.

A: What do you mean?

T: Well, the first humans lived in groups. Every group had a leader. The leader made the decisions about what the group should do. We now believe that originally, yawning might have been a signal from the leader that it was time to do something different. When the leader yawned, everybody else yawned, too—kind of in agreement.

A: Now I'm starting to yawn! You've started this!

T: Yes, I'm yawning, too.

A: Well, maybe it's time for a commercial break then…

Unit 10
1b-c

A = Amanda, T = Tiffany

T: Hello?

A: Tiffany…it's Amanda.

T: Oh, hi. Hey…is everything OK?

A: Yes… Well no, not really. I don't know where Daniel is. Nobody's seen him since lunchtime.

T: Isn't he at the office?

A: No. His secretary told me he left right after lunch, and he said he was going downtown, and he wouldn't be back. And then I called the downtown office, but they said he hadn't been there either. It's just so unlike him.

T: Do you think there's something wrong?

A: I really don't know what to think. He's been acting strangely recently, yes. It's like he's trying to hide something and…I don't know. Last week he told me he was working late, but I called the office, and they said he had gone out.

T: Hmm… . That's unlike Daniel.

A: Yes, it is. But the strangest thing happened last night.

T: Why, what happened?

A: Well, I was asking him what he was going to wear to Serena and Jim's wedding. It's next week. He said, "Oh, I don't know… . We may not be able to go." He wouldn't tell me what he meant. I didn't know what he was talking about. Of course we're going.

T: That sounds really odd. You'd better ask him what's going on.

A: You're right. I should.

D = Daniel, J = Jeff

J: OK. Here are your tickets.

D: Thanks.

J: Do you have your passports?

D: Yes.

J: Excellent. You're all set then.

D: Thanks a lot, Jeff.

J: Your wife still knows nothing?

D: Not a thing.

J: Well, she's going to get a big surprise!

D: I know. Thanks!

A = Amanda, D = Daniel

A: Daniel, what is all this about? What are these suitcases? Are you going somewhere? Why won't you tell me anything?

D: We're going to Paris, darling. Right now. Happy birthday.

A: Paris! Oh, Daniel! I've never been to Paris! And I've always wanted to go there.

D: And now you will. They say it's beautiful at this time of year.

A: But what about my clothes? I don't know what…I don't have any…

D: Don't worry about it. I packed for us!

A: Oh, my! I can't believe it!

D: I wanted it to be a surprise.

A: And it is! It's a wonderful surprise! Thank you so much! Oh, Daniel…you've been acting so strangely lately. I didn't know what was going on! I called your office and they said you weren't there…and…I…I had no idea… .

D: Oh, darling. Let's go! We'll miss the plane.

2c

M = Man, W = Woman

1

M: Have you ever been to the United States before?

W: Yes, I was here last year.

2

W: I'm looking for a coffee shop.

M: There's one on the second floor.

3

M: What time is it?

W: I don't know. I forgot my watch this morning.

4

W: Did you get the job?

M: They'll tell me tomorrow.

5a-b

E = Employee, G = Guest

G: What's this? I'm sorry. I don't think you understood what I meant.

E: You said you wanted a waiting room. This is the best place to wait for someone.

G: Oh, no! I didn't mean a **waiting** room. I meant a **weight** room. You know, a room with weights.

E: Oh, you mean, like a gym?

G: Yes!

E: Oh, I thought you said a **waiting** room! I'm sorry about that.

G: No problem.

E: OK…well, there is a gym on the third floor.

G: OK, thanks.

E: I thought it was kind of strange, asking for a waiting room in a hotel.

7b-c

M = Man, W1 = Woman 1, W2 = Woman 2

W1: You know, Bill always opens the car door for me. People don't usually do that these days.

W2: No, no, they certainly don't.

W1: I love it. I feel really special.

W2: Oh, I don't know. I don't think I like it very much. I mean, really…I can open the door for myself. I'm not helpless!

M: Remind me not to open the car door for you.

W2: Well, you wouldn't anyway! But I don't think it's really important to open car doors for people.

W1: You know, it's different when you're going through a door. Like yesterday, I was in a store, and this woman went through the door ahead of me, and she just let the door close in my face! She knew I was there!

M: That's so rude!

W2: It is! She should have apologized at least. That's what I would have done.

M: I always hold the door open for the person behind me.

W1: Well, I think that's basic good manners. But a lot of people don't have good manners any more.

W2: I agree. Certainly a lot of things that used to be considered good manners are going out of style.

M: Like what?

W2: Like writing thank-you notes, for example. I still do it, but a lot of people don't. People don't even expect it any more. Now, I write people a thank-you note and they say, "Wow, what a nice thing to do!" Like, they're really surprised. But my mother said, "Always write a thank-you note," so I do.

W1: You were brought up well!

W2: I guess I was.

W1: My parents always insisted that we call our friends' parents "Mr. Smith" or "Mrs. Sullivan" or whatever. So we did. When I got older, I always felt really strange doing that.

M: But I hardly ever use "mister" or "missus" anymore. Think about it. When was the last time you called someone "mister?"

W2: So many people use first names now.

W1: That's true, but sometimes I still don't know what name to use. Like the guy who owns the building next door. His name is Don McGinty. I never know whether to call him Don, or Mr. McGinty.

W2: Hmm…there's no real rule, is there?

Unit 11

5b-c

J = Jeannie, L = Lyle

J: Hey, listen to this. "A judge in Minnesota has sentenced some young people to listen to orchestras playing love songs."

L: What?

J: As a punishment. For playing loud rock music.

L: Why? How is that a punishment?

J: They were playing some kind of loud music—rock, or rap or something—in their cars. It was disturbing the neighbors, who called the police. So the judge gave them a choice between paying a fifty-dollar fine or listening to the style of music that they most disliked. It says here, "The judge sees her method as an effective way to make the teenagers consider their crime. 'If they are making people listen to their music, I will make them listen to mine,' she said."

L: Hah! I think that's a good idea.

J: I suppose so. Actually…I don't know if it would really be effective.

L: Well, it might make them see things from other people's point of view.

J: Yes. I guess that's why she did it.

L: It's like that landlord story a few weeks ago.

J: What was that about?

L: Well, this guy was in court because he was renting apartments that were in terrible condition—no heat, no water, or anything. His building was a mess. So the judge ordered him to live in his own building for a while.

J: Wow! Good idea!

L: He said he should experience the same conditions. And also, if he was living in it, it would ensure that the repairs got done.

J: It's better than going to prison.

L: Yes. Well, he could have gone to prison, otherwise. But this was a more practical solution.

J: Prison wouldn't have been as effective. At least this way, the repairs probably got done.

L: I agree. It seems more logical to make the punishment fit the crime.

J: I had a teacher once who believed in that idea.

L: Really?

J: When I was in seventh grade, I hated gym class, and I always tried to get out of it. My friend and I used to hide in the locker room during class. Well, eventually we were caught.

L: What happened?

J: We had to go to the library and do a whole project on physical fitness. We had to get statistics. For example, how many people in the population are overweight, why exercise is good for you…things like that. And we had to do it during gym class. Then we had to present it to the class.

L: That's really good. I bet you learned a lot.

J: Yes. I learned a lot, but I still hated gym!

9a-b

When I had just left high school, I was offered a job overseas for a year. But I wasn't sure that that was what I wanted. I was worried about going so far away, leaving my friends… you know. So I was talking to a friend of my father's about this, and he said, "Travel while you're young." It's a cliché, I know, but talking to him, I suddenly realized that I was going to be old one day and that I didn't want to realize then that I'd had a chance and not taken it. So I put off going to college, went overseas, and it turned out to be a fantastic experience. If he hadn't said that to me, I might never have gone.

My mother always said, "If something's bothering you, go for a walk by yourself." She used to do this all the time. We just accepted it as normal. Now I realize that she was doing that to get a chance to be by herself, and to think about things. And now I do what she did. Whenever I have a problem that I can't work out, I go out for a walk, and it always helps me feel better!

My grandmother had a mirror by the front door, and she always looked at herself in the mirror before she went out. It became a bit of a joke in the family, because the mirror was too high for her, and she had to stand on tiptoe to look in it. But she said, "Whatever you do, always check a mirror before you go out. You never know when you might have food stuck between your teeth!"

I was really shy, and I was nervous about going to a party where I didn't know anyone. And the friend that I was going with said, "Look, just ask questions. People aren't really interested in you. What they really want is to talk about themselves. Just keep on asking questions. Try to find out about them." I did, and it worked. And ever since then I've always done that whenever I meet new people, and it keeps the conversation going.

11a-b

H = Helga, I = Interviewer

I: Congratulations, Helga. You must be delighted to finally win the championship.

H: I am, yes! Thank you!

I: You've played really well this season.

H: Yes! Well, I think that injury I had last year really helped me in the end. I took a break, and my game was much stronger when I came back.

I: So it all turned out OK?

H: Yes, it did. I think it's because of the break that I played so well this season.

I: You had a new coach, too, right?

H: Yes, and I owe a lot to her. I couldn't have done it if she hadn't pushed so hard.

Unit 12
5a-b

1

H = Hannah, L = Lauren

H: Are you OK, Lauren? You look a little pale.

L: I don't feel very well. I think I'm coming down with something.

H: Why don't you go home early?

L: Yes. Maybe I will.

H: I hope you feel better.

L: Thanks.

2

J = John, K = Kay

K: How's Lauren?

J: Actually, she's not very well. She's been off work all week.

K: Oh dear. I hope it's nothing serious.

J: I don't think so. The doctor says she's a bit run down.

K: Well, give her my best wishes.

J: I will. Thanks.

3

J = John, K = Kay

K: How's Lauren?

J: Oh, she's feeling much better. She'll be back at work next week.

K: Oh, I'm glad to hear that.

7b-c

Ir = Interviewer, Ie = Interviewee

Ir: OK, now let me get this straight. You belong to a laughter club?

Ie: That's right.

Ir: That sounds hilarious.

Ie: It is! We laugh a lot.

Ir: Tell me about it.

Ie: Well, the idea started off a few years ago in India. A doctor named Madan Kataria came up with the idea. He began to think that people weren't laughing enough, so he just went up to people and said, do you want to start a laughing club? Of course everybody thought he was crazy. But he managed to start a club in a public park in Bombay.

Ir: I guess there is some evidence that laughter is good for you.

Ie: Yes, there is. Particularly in terms of relieving stress, but it also increases oxygen levels in the body, relieves pain…a lot of things. It's healthy. The other thing that Dr. Kataria says is that laughter is a social thing. In the clubs, we laugh together and it helps people connect with one another.

Ir: So that was the beginning…

Ie: Yes, and now there are hundreds of laughter clubs—a lot in India, but there are others in different countries all over the world.

Ir: Can anybody set up a laughter club?

Ie: Well, the leader of our club is certified. You can get trained to do it.

Ir: And what do you do in a laughter club? How do you start laughing? Do you tell jokes?

Ie: Not necessarily. They used to, but of course they ran out of jokes, so Dr. Kataria tried a different method. Now what we do is we start off with deep breathing exercises like this: "Ho-Ho-Ha-Ha." That usually starts everybody off.

Ir: And you just laugh?

Ie: Yes. There are different kinds of laughter and we have names for them all. There's silent laughter, hearty laughter, arm swinging laughter…and more. We do them all.

I: I still don't understand how you just start laughing, without a reason.

Ie: But that's just the thing. You don't need a reason to laugh. Any child can tell you that! You just have to look at someone laughing, and then you start. And then the more you laugh, the more reasons you find to laugh. Sometimes it's even hard to stop the session because we can't stop laughing!

13a

Number 1.

This is a school joke. A teacher is trying to teach some basic math, so he says to a little boy, "Now, Jimmy, if your father borrows ten dollars from me and pays me back one dollar a month, at the end of six months how much will he owe me?" And Jimmy says, "Ten dollars, sir." The teacher says, "I'm afraid you don't know much about math, Jimmy." And Jimmy says, ("I'm afraid you don't know much about my father, sir.")

Number 2.

My grandfather was walking down the street and he saw a little girl trying to reach the doorbell on a front door. It was very high, and she couldn't reach it. My grandfather wanted to help, so he went up to her and said "Let me do it, dear," and he rang the doorbell three times. "Great!" said the little girl. ("Now run as fast as you can!")

Number 3.

Little Susanna is watching her big sister cover her face with cream. "What's that for?" she asks. "To make me beautiful," says the sister. So Susanna watches as the sister wipes the cream off her face. She looks carefully at her sister's face and says, ("It doesn't work, does it?")

14a-b

When you're smiling, keep on smiling,
The whole world will smile with you;
And when you're laughing keep on laughing,
You'll find the sun will come shining through!
But when you're crying you bring on the rain;
Stop your sighing and be happy again.
When you're smiling, keep on smiling,
The whole wide world will smile with you!

Text Acknowledgments

The publishers are grateful to the individuals and institutions named below for permission to include their materials in this book.

p. 2: "Keeping in Touch" by Robert L. Humphrey. Excerpts from FACES' September 1996 issue: Communication, © 1996, Cobblestone Publishing, 30 Grove Street, Suite C, Peterborough, NH 03458. All Rights Reserved. Reprinted by permission of Carus Publishing Company.

p. 5: "Evolution, Alienation and Gossip" used by permission of Kate Fox/Social Issues Research Centre. Published online at www.sirc.org/publik/gossip.shtml.

p. 11: "Prince Eyango Aims His Songs at the Soul–and the Feet" by John Roos. Published May 13, 2000. Copyright, 2000, Los Angeles Times. Reprinted with permission.

p. 13: "A Time Traveler Returns, Still Restless" by Jane Gross (November 24, 1999). Copyright © 1999 by The New York Times Co. Reprinted with permission.

pp. 17, 18: Adapted version of the story "Table for Two" by Lori Peikoff. Copyright © by Lori Peikoff from I THOUGHT MY FATHER WAS GOD from NPR's National Story Project edited and introduced by Paul Auster. Reprinted with permission of the Carol Mann Agency.

p. 21: "Six degrees of separation not real spam" by George Ayoub, Columnist, The Grand Island Independent (2/15/02).

p. 24: **Bus Stop**
Words and Music by Graham Gouldman
© 1966 (Renewed 1994) MAN-KEN MUSIC LTD. and BRAMSDENE MUSIC CORP.
All Rights for the U.S. Controlled and Administered by EMI BLACKWOOD MUSIC INC.
All Rights Reserved   International Copyright Secured
Used by Permission

p. 27: "Every Job Has a Key Question: What's Yours?" by Richard Roeper, syndicated column Chicago Sun-Times. Published in The Arizona Republic, July 28, 2000, p. B9. Copyright © 2000, Richard Roeper. Reprinted by permission. Distributed by New York Times Special Features.

p. 28: Definitions for *risk, involve,* and *pretend.* Dictionary entries based on the Oxford ESL Dictionary (0-19-431683-1). Published in 2004.

p. 31: "10 Worst Jobs" by Chris Wood. Used by permission of the author and www.4jobs.com.

p. 33: Reprinted with the permission of Scribner, an imprint of Simon & Schuster Adult Publishing Group, from 'TIS by Frank McCourt. Copyright © 1999 by Frank McCourt.

p. 33: Reprinted with the permission of The Aaron M. Priest Literary Agency from 'TIS by Frank McCourt. Copyright © 1999 by Frank McCourt.

OXFORD
UNIVERSITY PRESS

198 Madison Avenue
New York, NY 10016 USA

Great Clarendon Street
Oxford OX2 6DP England

Oxford New York
Auckland Cape Town Dar es Salaam Hong Kong Karachi
Kuala Lumpur Madrid Melbourne Mexico City Nairobi
New Delhi Shanghai Taipei Toronto
With offices in
Argentina Austria Brazil Chile Czech Republic France Greece
Guatemala Hungary Italy Japan South Korea Poland Portugal
Singapore Switzerland Thailand Turkey Ukraine Vietnam

OXFORD is a trademark of Oxford University Press.

ISBN-13: 978 0 19 453685 1
ISBN-10: 0 19 453685 8

Copyright © 2004 Oxford University Press

Library of Congress Cataloging-in-Publication Data

Blackwell, Angela.
  English knowhow. Student book 3 / Angela Blackwell, Therese Naber ;
  with Gregory J. Manin.
    p. cm.
  ISBN-13: 978 0 19 453685 1 (pbk.)
  ISBN-10: 0 19 453685 8
  1. English language—Textbooks for foreign speakers. I. Title:
English knowhow student book 3. II. Naber, Therese. III. Manin, Gregory
J. IV. Title.
  PE1128 .B584 2004
  428.2'4—dc22

                        2003069125

Editorial Manager: Judith A. Cunningham
Editors: Margaret Brooks, Kathryn L. O'Dell
Assistant Editors: Melinda M. Beck, Alexis Vega-Singer
Design Project Manager: Maria Epes
Senior Designer: Claudia Carlson
Art Editors: Judi DeSouter, Justine Eun
Production Manager: Shanta Persaud
Production Controller: Zainaltu Jawat Ali

Printing (last digit): 10 9 8 7 6 5 4

Printed in Hong Kong.

Acknowledgments

Cover photographs: Geri Engberg (woman with book); International Stock/ImageState (airport); Stephen Ogilvy (man with certificate); PictureArts Corporation (trophy)

Illustrations: Matthew Archambault pp. 7 (people), 60 (woman), 71 (woman); Barbara Bastian pp. 11 (article), 13 (article), 33 (extract), 37 (article), 41 (article), 45 (article), 53 (article), 69 (article), 85 (article), 91 (article), 95 (article), 100 (article); Kathy Baxendale p. 2 (article), 18 (story), 57 (letter), 64 (letter); Annie Bissett p. 21 (article), 66 (ads), 84 (situations); Carmelo Blandino p. 16 (topics); Paul Casale pp. 29 (men), 50 (TV show), 63 (people); Lyndall Culbertson pp. 28 (directions), 32 (memo), 35 (article), 36 (headlines), 38 (notes), 47 (dictionary), 54 (notes), 60 (song), 61 (flyer, business card), 67 (articles), 75 (quiz), 82 (survey), 89 (headlines); Patrick Faricy pp. 38 (canoeing), 82 (lobby); Linda Fong pp. 19 (itinerary), 24 (song), 85 (haiku), 86 (haiku), 101 (note paper); Martha Gavin pp. 1 (street), 72 (people); Yvonne Gilbert pp. 45 & 46 (folk tale characters); Paul Hampson pp. 4 (cartoon), 87 (robbery); Rob Hefferan pp. 12 (campfire), 56 (people), 94 (people), 98 (people); Rosanne Kaloustian p. 17 (Milky Way); Uldis Klavins pp. 21 (package), 58 (car parts), 63 (cup, jeans, faucet, tie, shirt, car); Arnie Levin pp. 14 (hobby), 76 (yawns), 103 (people); Rose Marie Lowry p. 55 (landmarks); Angelo Tillery pp. 5 (people), 40 (warning), 97 (people); Fred Willingham pp. 31 (on air), 65 (people)

Commissioned photographs: Carol Balistreri/Oxford University Press p. 20 (men), Stephen Ogilvy pp. 17 (books), 67 (sandwich board), 79 (couple, men, woman)

The publishers would like to thank the following for their permission to reproduce photographs: Lori Adamski Peek/Getty Images p. 107 (tree); AFP/Corbis pp. 108 (people), 110 (people); AFP/Getty Images p. 61 (Cinemobil); Steve Allen/Brand X Pictures/PictureQuest p. 55 (dome); AP Photos p. 53 (tunnel); Bill Bachman/Index Stock p. 42 (mountains); BananaStock/SuperStock p. 102 (people); Charles Barsotti/CartoonBank p. 112 (clown, receptionist); Paul Barton/CORBIS p. 111 (people); Alistair Berg/Photodisc/Getty Images p. 81 (photo A); Bettmann/CORBIS pp. 41 (lava, town), 43 (runner), 54 (bridge), 100 (men); Angela Blackwell pp. 9 (accordion), 62 (signs); Charles Bowman/age fotostock p. 56 (at night); Ron Brown/age fotostock p. 96 (pharmacy); In-House Rendering/Claudia Carlson p. 11 (prince); Matthew Cavanaugh p. 99 (women); Tom Cheney/CartoonBank p. 34 (skeleton); Michael Cogliantry/Getty Images p. 100 (sleeping); Peter Correz/Getty Images p. 17 (header); Ed Fisher/CartoonBank p. 34 (robot); Fotos & Photos/Index Stock p. 42 (desert); Owen Franken/CORBIS p. 58 (Citroen); Jean Freibert/Index Stock p. 27 (chef); William Fritsch/PictureQuest p. 90 (judge); Ewing Galloway/Index Stock p. 2 (pony express); Shelley Gazin/CORBIS p. 15 (TV show); Jeff Greenberg/Index Stock p. 53 (header); Bob Handelman/Getty Images p. 25 (studio); Sidney Harris/CartoonBank p. 112 (dentist); John & Dallas Heaton/CORBIS p. 2 (alphorn); John Henley/CORBIS p. 22 (student); Ralf-Finn Hestoft/SABA/CORBIS p. 61 (gym); C. Mike Hettwer, Courtesy of Project Exploration p. 73 (fossil, man); Jack Hollingsworth/Photodisc/Getty Images p. 81 (photo C); Honshu-Shikoku Bridge Authority p. 53 (bridge); Image Source Ltd/Alamy p. 87 (header); ImageSource/elektraVision/PictureQuest p. 91 (men); ImageState/Alamy p. 55 (fountain); Chris Ison/PA Photos p. 3 (bird); David Joel/age fotostock p. 96 (surgeons); Lou Jones/Index Stock p. 27 (header); Adele Keeley p. 27 (designer); Layne Kennedy/CORBIS p. 37 (ranger); Lucille Khornak/Index Stock Imagery/PictureQuest p. 96 (boy); Knopf Publishing/Random House p. 13 (book cover); Edward Koren/CartoonBank p. 34 (sunset); Bud Kraft p. 61 (pool); Dennis Macdonald/Index Stock p. 107 (pollution); Anthony Marsland/Getty Images p. 1 (header); Wally McNamee/CORBIS p. 43 (header); Omar Mediano - www.marfalights.com p. 69 (sign); Anthony Meshkinyar/Getty Images p. 68 (radio); Mark Miller/Index Stock p. 69 (ruins); Warren Miller/CartoonBank p. 74 (cartoon); Colin Monteath/age fotostock p. 36 (horses); Paul Morse/Retna p. 13 (man); Musicians On Call p. 95 (musicians); PBNJ Productions/CORBIS p. 79 (header); Jose Luis Pelaez/CORBIS p. 85 (hands); Photodisc/Getty Images p. 35 (header); PhotoLink/Photodisc/PictureQuest p. 55 (monument); plainpicture/Alamy p. 31 (cowgirl); Michael Prince/CORBIS p. 95 (header); Jose Fuste Raga/CORBIS p. 87 (dome); Steve Raymer/CORBIS p. 9 (header); Richard Harding Picture Library Ltd/Alamy p. 48 (star); Rolf Richardson/Alamy p. 37 (sign); Galen Rowell/CORBIS p. 51 (avalanche); Royalty-Free/CORBIS p. 22 (nurse); Courtesy of Robert M. Schoch p. 77 (ruins); Bernard Schoebaum/CartoonBank p. 100 (cartoon); Bob Shomler p. 9 (performing); Cover from THE CLUE OF THE BROKEN LOCKET by Carolyn Keene/Simon and Schuster p. 43 (detective); Frank McCourt/Simon and Schuster p. 33 (book cover); ML Sinibladi/CORBIS p. 69 (rocks); Ariel Skelley/CORBIS p. 27 (saleswoman); Mark Smith/The Herald & Weekly Times Limited p. 35 (penguin); Joe Sohm, Chromosohm/Stock Connection/PictureQuest p. 48 (cameras); doug steley/Alamy p. 43 (boat); James Stevenson/CartoonBank p. 34 (good work); Tom Stewart/CORBIS p. 31 (seaman); Stock Connection, Inc./Alamy p. 31 (roofer); Stockbyte/PictureQuest p. 22 (software developer); Harald Sund/Getty Images p. 69 (header); SW Productions/Photodisc/Getty Images p. 81 (photo B); Chase Swift/CORBIS p. 48 (red carpet); Paul Trummer/Getty Images p. 56 (day); Peter Turnley/CORBIS p. 27 (stock trader); Jorge Tutor p. 57 (plaza); Steve Vidler/eStock Photography/PictureQuest p. 42 (harbor); Aneal Vohra/Index Stock p. 61 (header); Tom Wagner/CORBIS SABA p. 22 (journalist); Jennifer Weisbord/NY Post p. 67 (motion ad); From "Building Big" at www.pbs.org/wgbh/buildingbig Copyright © 2000 WGBH/Boston p. 53 (dam); David Woodfall/Getty Images p. 107 (trash); Brian Yarvin/age fotostock p. 43 (father); David Young-Wolff/PhotoEdit/PictureQuest p. 27 (toll booth)

Special thanks to: Erin Neff p. 9 (singer); Franco Balistreri and Benedetto Ingallina p. 20 (friends); Cindy Muzio p. 24 (advice and support); Curt Maloney p. 58 (truck and rambler photos); Psyche Kennett p. 60 (advice and support); James Jay Racheff, Jr. p. 67 (sandwich board model); Professor Elof Axel Carlson p. 91 (story)

The authors and publishers extend thanks to the following English Language Teaching professionals and institutions for their invaluable support and feedback during the development of this series: Gill Adams (Brazil); Virgílio Almeida and staff (Brazil); Barbara Bangle (Mexico); Jocélia Pizzamiglio Basso and staff (Brazil); Vera Berk (Brazil); James Boyd (Japan); Bonnie Brown de Masis (Costa Rica); Janaína Cardoso and staff (Brazil); Hector Castillo (Mexico); Dr. Robin Chapman (Japan); Ana Isabel Delgado (Brazil); Nora Díaz (Mexico); Maria da Graça Duarte and staff (Brazil); Stephen Edmunds (Mexico); Israel Escalante (Mexico); Raquel Faria and staff (Brazil); Verónica Galván (Mexico); Saul Santos García (Mexico); Carmen Gehrke and staff (Brazil); Arlete Würschig Gonçalves and staff (Brazil); Kimberley Humphries (Mexico); Michelle Johnstone (Canada); Sonya Kozicki-Jones (Costa Rica); Jean-Pierre Louvrier (Brazil); Shan-jen Amy Lu (Taiwan); Mary Meyer (Paraguay); Dulce Montes de Oca (Mexico); Harold Murillo (Colombia); Connie Reyes (Mexico); Carmen Oliveira and staff (Brazil); Joselanda de Oliveira and staff (Brazil); Thelma Félix Oliveira (Brazil); Ane Cibele Palma and staff (Brazil); Eliane Cunha Peixoto and staff (Brazil); Verónica Olguín (Mexico); Claudia Otake (Mexico); Nicola Sarjeant (Korea); Débora Schisler and staff (Brazil); Lilian Munhoz Soares and staff (Brazil); Sharon Springer (Costa Rica); Sílvia Thalacker and staff (Brazil); Kris Vicca (Taiwan); Ignacio Yepes and staff (Mexico); Daniel Zarate (Mexico); Mirna Züge (Brazil).
Centro Cultural Brasil-Estados Unidos, Santos; Centro de Línguas Estrangeiras Mackenzie, São Paulo; ENEP Acatlán, Edo. de México; English Forever, Salvador; Escola Técnica Estadual Fernando Prestes, Sorocaba; English Forever, Salvador; IBEU, Fortaleza; IBEU, Rio; Instituto Cultural Brasileiro Norte-Americano, Porto Alegre; Interamericano-CCBEU, Curitiba; MAI, Belo Horizonte; Plus!, Brasília; Quatrum, Porto Alegre; SENAC, Rio; Seven, São Paulo; Talkative, São Paulo; Universidad Autónoma de México; Universidad Autónoma del Estado de México; Universidade Católica de Brasília; Universidade de Caxias do Sul-PLE; Universidad La Salle, León, Guanajuato; Universidad Latino Americano, Mexico City; Universidad Nacíonal Autónoma de México; Universidad Autónoma de Guadalajara.